THE EYE OF

C000183410

THE EYE OF THE NEEDLE

THE EYE
OF THE
NEEDLE

**No Salvation Outside the Poor:
A Utopian–Prophetic Essay**[1]

JON SOBRINO

Translated by Dinah Livingstone

Introduction by Michael Campbell-Johnston SJ

DARTON · LONGMAN + TODD

First published in 2008 by
Darton, Longman and Todd Ltd
1 Spencer Court
140–142 Wandsworth High Street
London SW18 4JJ

ISBN 10: 0–232–52739–3
ISBN 13: 978–0–232–52739–1

A catalogue record for this book is available from
the British Library.

Designed and produced by Sandie Boccacci
Set in 11/13.5pt Utopia
Printed and bound in Great Britain by
Athenaeum Press, Gateshead, Tyne & Wear

CONTENTS

INTRODUCTION 7

1. WE MUST CHANGE THE COURSE OF HISTORY 17

2. A VERY SICK WORLD 21

3. THE POOR AND SALVATION 41

4. EXTRA PAUPERES NULLA SALUS 75

5. THE MYSTERY OF THE POOR 79

NOTES 86

INTRODUCTION

A Preferential Option for the Poor became an accepted part of ecclesiastical jargon and policy in the 1980s. This was largely due to the two conferences of Latin American bishops at Medellin in 1968 and Puebla in 1979 which profoundly influenced the universal Church. The first, though it did not use the expression, recognised that 'a deafening cry pours from the throats of millions of men, asking their pastors for a liberation that reaches them from nowhere else' (14.2). From this came the commitment 'to make ours their problems and their struggles' (14.10). The second declared formally the need 'for conversion on the part of the whole Church to a preferential option for the poor, an option aimed at their integral liberation' (1134).

The way was also prepared by the 1971 Synod of Bishops on *Justice in the World* which again, without using the formula, recognised 'the Church's vocation to be present in the heart of the world by proclaiming the Good News to the poor, freedom to the oppressed and joy to the afflicted' (5). And it confirmed the right of the poor to take their future into their own hands and the Church's duty to give witness to justice by first being just herself.

The option was taken up by many religious congregations. In 1983 the Jesuits adopted it at their 33rd General Congregation in these words:

> The validity of our mission will also depend to
> a large extent on our solidarity with the poor.
> For though obedience sends us, it is poverty
> that makes us believable. So, together with
> many other religious congregations, we wish
> to make our own the Church's preferential
> option for the poor. This option is a decision
> to love the poor preferentially because there is
> a desire to heal the whole human race. Such
> love, like Christ's own, excludes no one but
> neither does it excuse anyone from its
> demands. Directly or indirectly, this option
> should find some concrete expression in
> every Jesuit's life, in the orientation of our
> existing apostolic works, and in our choice of
> new ministries. (52)

Four years later, this option was extended official-
ly to the whole Church by Pope John Paul II in his
Encyclical *Sollicitudo Rei Socialis*. It is within the
context of this development that Jon Sobrino's lat-
est book needs to be placed and understood. Its
origins, however, go back much further, to the
ground-breaking work in Central America of his
close friend and mentor Ignacio Ellacuría, rector
of the Central American University and one of the
six Jesuits massacred there in 1989.

For the Jesuits of Central America, Ellacuría was
responsible more than anyone else for opening
their eyes to the challenges of Vatican II and their
implementation in the Society's work and life
through the decrees of its 32nd General
Congregation in 1974. He gave a controversial

retreat to the young Jesuits of the Province, urging them to break away from restrictive structures so as to reach out to and identify with the ordinary people. Until removed by outside pressures, he was appointed their formation superior. But it was above all, during his long stint as rector of the Central American University (UCA), that he showed what a genuine option for the poor was and where it should lead, and this in a private university, an institution that in Latin America traditionally catered for the middle and upper classes.

Jon Sobrino freely acknowledges his influence, quoting him at the start and conclusion of this present work and many times throughout it. To some extent it represents an updating of Ellacuría's ideas and their application to our world of today. He himself describes its central theme as a recognition that, 'in order to heal a civilisation that is very sick, we need, in some form, *the input of the poor and the victims'*. To achieve this, Sobrino takes and develops two key ideas of Ellacuría.

The first is his bold concept of a 'civilisation of poverty' in which he argues that poverty is not just a counsel of perfection but also an historical necessity. Our world today is profoundly sick because the civilisation of wealth or capital that dominates it cannot be extended to what a recent writer has called 'the bottom billion' of the poor. It cannot be denied it has brought many benefits to humanity which should be preserved and furthered, but it is equally clear that there are not enough material resources on earth to let all countries achieve the same level of production and consumption as that of the countries called wealthy, which are inhabited by less than 25 per cent of the world's population. One is reminded of Mahatma Gandhi's reply to a journalist who asked him if the newly independent India would now attain the same living standards as the British, their previous colonial masters: 'It took Britain half the resources of this planet to achieve its prosperity; how many planets do you think a country like India would require?' It follows that, if the behaviour and even the ideal of a few cannot become the behaviour and reality of the greater part of humanity, then it cannot be said to be moral or even human, all the more so if the enjoyment of the few is at the cost of depriving the rest.

But not only can this ideal not be realised, it is not even desirable. This because in the last analysis, as Ellacuría points out, it proposes:

> the private accumulation of the greatest possible capital on the part of individuals, groups, multinationals, states or groups of states as the fundamental basis of development, and individuals' or families' possessive accumulation of the most possible wealth as the fundamental basis for their own security and for the possibility of ever growing consumption as the basis of their own happiness.

This is not only un-Christian but dehumanising, as Sobrino clearly explains.

Hence the need for a civilisation of poverty 'whose guiding principle is the universal satisfaction of basic needs' and the 'growth of shared solidarity as fundamental to the making of humanity'.

Ellacuría was at pains to point out this does not mean the penury or destitution presently suffered by so many that must be condemned as a scandal and disgrace, but rather a new civilisation enabling all to have access to the material and cultural goods that make for a truly human life. This would inevitably reduce the enormous and growing gap between those who have and those who haven't. It would also be fully coherent with the teaching of Jesus. 'It cannot be denied, without suppressing essential elements of the gospel, that wealth is a great obstacle to Christian liberty and that poverty is a great support for that liberty. The idea of having more as a condition for being more is a diabolical temptation, rejected by Jesus at the start of his public mission'.

Is this all pie in the sky, an unrealisable utopia? Ellacuría clearly didn't think so since he suggested a number of specific measures that could lead towards it. These would affect the role of human work in society, the ownership of property, the satisfaction of basic needs, political structures that promote community and individual initiative, religious structures that grow upwards from the base, and a new cultural order. But all of them would depend on a conversion whose first step is to look at the world through the eyes of the poor and begin to understand it in a different way. A second condition is that a civilisation of poverty calls for new attitudes towards wealth and possessions that will only be possible to achieve through a radical change in lifestyles. It could well be that an additional incentive for this might now be the effects of the climate change that is looming ahead.

The second key idea of Ellacuría, which Sobrino develops considerably in this essay and holds to be its main contribution, is that of a 'crucified people' who need to participate directly and actively in their own liberation for this to come about at all. It is not something that can be achieved without them or by outsiders. Others can help and contribute to the process in a variety of ways, but it has to start and be directed by the poor themselves. For this reason, in a telling phrase, Ellacuría describes those involved as 'the poor with spirit' who will be the ones to play a determining role in creating a civilisation of solidarity rather than selfishness.

This view is increasingly supported by development economists and aid experts. There is a growing awareness that many aid programmes have failed precisely because they were imposed on poor countries by international agencies and financing governments without taking into account the real needs and desires of the poor themselves. A recent study, *The White Man's Burden* by William Easterly (OUP, 2006), admits openly that planners have drawn up numerous 'solutions' which have in fact done more harm than good. And it concludes: 'Only the self-reliant efforts of poor people and poor societies themselves can end poverty, borrowing ideas and institutions from the West when it suits them to do so' (p. 334). In *The Bottom Billion* (OUP, 2007), Paul Collier, former Director of Development Research at the World Bank, addresses the issue of 'why poorer countries are failing', and pinpoints four major problems that trap them in structures they have not created, and from which the wealthy and powerful, often abetted by the World Bank and the International Monetary Fund, prevent them from escaping. He also insists several times that 'the society of the bottom billion can only be rescued from within' (pp. xi, 12, 96). And in words strongly reminiscent of Ellacuría's 'poor with spirit', he claims that:

> In every society of the bottom billion there are people working for change, but usually they are defeated by the powerful internal forces stacked against them. We should be helping the heroes. So far, our efforts have been paltry: through inertia, ignorance, and incompetence, we have stood by and watched them lose (p. 96).

This, of course, does not mean canonising the poor. There is no reason to believe that many are any less venal, corrupt or egoistic than the non-poor. But experience has often shown that some are generous with the little they have and often prepared to help others in worse conditions than themselves. It is also true that the loss of human possessions can encourage a certain detachment from material things. As someone has put it, if you take away everything from a person, that person becomes free. So Ellacuría claims the crucified people are like a mirror in which the First World sees itself the other way round and recognises the truth about itself which otherwise it tries to hide.

Sobrino is probably correct in claiming that his formula *extra pauperes nulla salus* ('no salvation outside – or apart from – the poor') is something new that does not appear in any modern texts. But a genuine option for the poor has always, in my opinion, recognised it is from the poor themselves that liberation must start and be developed. In their 32nd general congregation already referred to above, the Jesuits recognised this clearly:

> If we have the patience and the humility and the courage to walk with the poor, we will learn from what they have to teach us what we can do to help them. Without this arduous journey, our efforts for the poor will have an effect just the opposite from what we intend. We will only hinder them from getting a hearing for their real wants and from acquiring the means of taking charge of their own destiny, personal and collective. (4, 50)

I do not find Sobrino's formula an unexpected novelty, and certainly don't think it is scandalous.

But more important is the detailed study he gives it in the second part of this essay, and its application to reality when dealing with kinds of salvation, the historical forms of salvation coming from the world of the poor, and the role of the non-poor. One is tempted to ask whether the sufferings of a crucified people, though crying to heaven for vengeance, have in themselves a redemptive value as St Paul claims that 'by means of my physical sufferings, I am helping to complete what still remains of Christ's sufferings on behalf of his body, the church' (Col 1:24).

Be that as it may, my own experiences in El Salvador of the poor and innocent suffering severe persecution and violence in a cruel civil war for which they had little or no responsibility convinces me we have a lot to learn from this crucified people. I shall never forget a mother in one of the refugee camps who had just got news that one of her sons had been killed. An eyewitness, herself wounded, related how the soldiers had cut off his hands and feet, slashed his face and partially skinned him before he died. The mother, quiet and dignified in her grief, didn't even know which of her two remaining sons were involved: a 12-year-old or his 14-year-old brother. While she spoke, two of her little daughters played on the ground and one slept in my lap, blissfully unaware of their brother's horrible fate. Yet, during the Holy Week services that followed, the mother and many others forgave and prayed for those who had tortured and murdered their children or parents. Of such is the Kingdom of heaven and in such our hope for a new world.

Michael Campbell-Johnston SJ

1. WE MUST CHANGE THE COURSE OF HISTORY

On 6 November 1989 Ignacio Ellacuría gave a speech in Barcelona. As it turned out, it was a programme, as well the last speech he ever made:

> Together with all the poor and oppressed people in the world, we need utopian hope to encourage us to believe we can change the course of history. And not only change its course, but subvert it and set it going in another direction [...] On another occasion I talked about a 'coprohistorical analysis', that is, the examination of our civilisation's faeces. This examination seems to show that our civilisation is very sick. To escape from such a dire prognosis, we must try to change it from within.[2]

That very sick civilisation is the *capital-civilisation,* which Ellacuría also called the *wealth-civilisation.* It makes 'the accumulation of capital the driving force of history; it considers the possession and enjoyment of capital to be what makes us human.'[3] It has offered no adequate solution to the basic needs lacked by most people on this planet, neither has it accorded them human fellowship. The conclusion is clear: 'in a world driven wrong by the dynamic of capital and wealth, we need to set up a counter-dynamic to stop it and save the world from it.'[4]

This new dynamic arises from a *work-civilisation*, which he also called a *poverty-civilisation*. 'It is based on a materialist humanism lit by Christian inspiration; its guiding principle is the universal satisfaction of basic needs and it sees the growth of shared solidarity as fundamental to the making of humanity.'[5]

Of course, Ellacuría insisted that we should hold on to all the important achievements of our present historical moment: scientific research, which has improved various aspects of life; our ethical and cultural progress in human rights, and other ideological and cultural advances, such as certain elements of modern democracies. So 'stop' and 'save' do not mean 'starting from scratch' but do mean 'starting again' and 'starting against' the principles that govern our present wealth-civilisation.

For Ellacuría the evils needing to be overcome were obvious: poverty, worsening exploitation, the scandalous gap between rich and poor, ecological destruction, as well as the perversion of actual advances in democracy and the ideological manipulation of human rights ... He spoke out repeatedly against *dehumanisation,* the degradation and prostitution of spirit, about which too little was, and still is, being said. We have only to recall his criticism in his Barcelona speech of 'the dehumanisation of people who give up the struggle to become and *be,* for the sake of the all-out pursuit of producing and *having,* accumulating wealth, power and honour and an ever-increasing range of consumer goods'.[6] That is the specific dehumanisation produced by a capital-civilisation. It is very serious, and it is everywhere.

To overcome this wealth-civilisation and its evils, Ellacuría urges us to 'raise collective aware-ness calling for radical changes ... and to create economic, political and cultural models to allow capital-civilisation to be replaced by a work-civilisation.'[7] Both these tasks are necessary and both very difficult indeed. To make them happen, he urgently recommends utopian vision and hope 'with all the poor and oppressed people in the world'.[8] That gives us the central theme of this essay: in order to heal a civilisation that is very sick, we need, in some form, *the input of the poor and the victims.*

2. A VERY SICK WORLD

We have recalled Ellacuría's words spoken in 1989. What about today? Certainly, history has brought about important new developments. From a historical viewpoint, René Girard thinks that we are seeing the birth of a kinder humanity, that is more concerned for the victims: 'No society has ever been as concerned about the victims as ours is.'[9] However, he believes this is 'really only a show of concern';[10] he does not want to 'call the world we live in blameless'[11] But he does insist that 'it is an unprecedented phenomenon'.[12] It could be something like what happened in the axial age, from the eighth to the sixth centuries BC, as described by Jaspers. And, despite his strong criticism, which we quote below, Dom Pedro Casaldáliga says that 'humanity is "on the move" and turning towards truth and justice. There is a lot of utopian hope and a lot of commitment on this sad planet.'[13] Nevertheless, today we are still deep in a *capital-civilisation*, which causes extreme want, dehumanises and attacks the human family: it excludes and impoverishes people and divides the world into winners and losers. Our civilisation continues to be 'very sick'. As Jean Ziegler puts it, its life – both its material and spiritual life – is 'under threat of death'. [14]

The wrongs suffered by the majority: injustice, cruelty and death

There is more wealth on Earth, but also more injustice. Africa has been called 'the world's dungeon', a continental *Shoah*. According to the Food and Agriculture Organisation of the United Nations (FAO),[15] 2,500 million people survive on Earth on less than two euros a day, and every day 25,000 people die of hunger. Desertification threatens the lives of 1,200 million people in about a hundred different countries (Bishop Pedro Casaldáliga).[16]

Sometimes we hear that our present globalised world offers new life chances to poor people, through migration. We should not rule this out or deny that migration may alleviate some evils, when people are driven to it by necessity. But today migration is not a simple readjustment of the human species – which has occurred throughout history and can be potentially enriching. Migrations today are particularly cruel because of how and why they happen. Let us quote Casaldáliga again:

> Immigrants are denied human fellowship and even the ground on which to stand. The United States is building a 1,500 kilometre wall against Latin America; while Europe is putting up a barrier against Africa in the south of Spain. As well as being iniquitous, this is all part of a programme. In a horrifying letter, written 'behind separating walls', one African

immigrant warns: 'I beg you not to think that it is normal for us to live this way; because in fact, the cause is the ongoing injustice built into the inhuman systems that kill and impoverish people [...] Do not support that system by your silence.[17]

Without batting an eyelid, we carry on in this crazy, shameless way, that is unjust, cruel, contemptuous and insulting. And we often cover up what we do. Here are a few thoughts:

- Worldwide spending on arms and armies in 2006 was a staggering 3.3 billion dollars a day,[18] while the total value of support to agriculture in rich countries still runs at over a billion dollars a day.[19]
- The arms trade is one of the most profitable for all governments in the international community. Together with China, the G8 countries account for 90 per cent of arms exports. At least half a million people are killed annually by small arms (Amnesty International).[20]
- The aim of globalisation is to dominate the rest of us, any other country, any other world [...] Globalisation is simply westernisation. The West wants to be the centre of the world (Aminata Traoré).[21]

Directly or indirectly, hunger, weapons, forced migrations through lack of land, water or soil, result in *death*. There are also diseases such as AIDS and malaria, which in one way or another lead to death, with the scandalous complicity of the multinational pharmaceutical companies, who have sought to protect their own patents by lobbying against making much cheaper life-saving generic treatments available.[22] Then there are many other sources of suffering, such as unemployment and social exclusion. None of these belongs to the order of nature. Their causes are historical. And it is important to recognise that today the fundamental cause is capitalism.

> 'Real capitalism' is responsible for the organisation of the world economy that is ethically and morally wrong, for the shameful and absurd coexistence in an ever more integrated world of appalling poverty with unprecedented wealth.[23]

All this happens today without being noticed.[24] When there is criticism, it focuses more on the *adjective* – such as *savage* capitalism – rather than on capitalism itself and its governing principle: *the right to property*.[25] As long as that principle is held to be absolute and unassailable, any economy in the world will be structurally configured by a dynamic of oppression; humans beings will be rated according to their ability to produce wealth; their right to possess and enjoy wealth will prolong and add to the oppression of others and, of course, widen the gap between the haves and have-nots.

Ultimately, this is a *cruel* society. It is cruel because of the suffering it inflicts on the oppressed, and because of its unfeeling attitude (although there are valiant exceptions) towards that suffering in a world of abundance. Leonardo Boff says: 'When future generations judge our time, they will call us barbarians, inhuman and pitiless, because of our heartlessness towards the sufferings of our brothers and sisters.'[26] To give just one example: 'If human beings had even a little humanity, just 4 per cent of the 225 largest fortunes in the world would be enough to give food, water, health and education to all.'[27] That is obscene.

We could go on quoting indefinitely.[28] The figures we have given refer to today, not to some pre-globalisation period and they come from responsible and informed sources. But if we want them to help heal our civilisation's 'serious illness', we must heed the warning of a Colombian missionary who has spent eighteen years in Uganda: 'Statistics don't bleed; people do.'

We are always seeking excuses to avoid confronting – or even coming into contact with – reality. Looking back, we might say that fifty years ago there was more wretched poverty on the planet, and in a sense that is true. But we must tell the whole truth; that is the only honest way to face reality. [29] Looking to the future, there might even be a sense of euphoria: within two decades China may be able to eliminate the hunger of hundreds of millions of people[30] – although we do not know whether they will manage it, or if they do, at what human cost.[31]

But even if we are optimistic, reality still screams at us. 'It can't be like this!'[32] 'God is angry.'[33] 'The unreasonable has become reasonable.'[34] And we haven't even mentioned Afghanistan, Iraq, Somalia, Darfur ...

Woes of the spirit suffered by human beings: dehumanisation

All this turns the vast majority in our world into 'crucified people, [...] whose human face continues to be wiped out by the sin of the world. The powers of that world keep robbing them of everything, snatching their life from them, yes above all, their life.'[35]

Ellacuría stresses the attack on life and that is where we began. The wealth-civilisation does not produce life; to a greater or lesser extent, it produces various kinds of death. Neither does it humanise people, which is what we want to focus on now. It is *inhuman* to deprive others of life when it would be possible to ensure it. But even more inhuman is the way that it is done, unjustly, cruelly and contemptuously – sometimes even in the name of a god. And it is inhuman that this deprivation of life should go hand in hand with the head-on pursuit of success and affluence. The wealth-civilisation fosters thinking and feeling that create a cultural and ideological climate poisoning the air the human spirit breathes. So not only is the *oikos* – our fundamental life-web – sick and in need of healing, but also the very *air* our spirits breathe. We are dehumanised, because we forget the *truth*. There is a *cover-up* of the truth and a proliferation of lies, *silence* in the face of scandalous inequality between rich and poor, *numbness* of the rich – and also of the poor – generated and indeed intended by the mass media.

It is dehumanising to forget *decency.* It is a brazen *mockery* of the victims to fail to implement important UN resolutions on fundamental human rights. There is massive *corruption* in nearly all spheres of power, justified by the unquestioned dogma of profit. There is *impunity* before, during and after atrocities, often carried out by governments themselves. It is also wrong to turn western democracy into an *absolute dogma,* without checking how it operates. [36]

It is dehumanising to forget *maturity,* especially now when we hear that our world has 'come of age'. There are *forms of fundamentalism,* that look attractive but have serious consequences: individualism, superficiality, success and pleasure are heedlessly accepted, promoted and rewarded. Simplistic and infantile attitudes are sometimes expressed with sentimental language in politics, and particularly often, in religion.

Then there is the dehumanising *compliance* of the West with Empire – *imperium magnum latrocinium* (the 'great thieving empire'), as Augustine called it, even if we don't talk like that much nowadays. This servility, in one form or another, makes the West an accomplice in that Empire's economic and military crimes and its human rights violations. It accepts the arrogance and domination of some human beings over others as normal. And it accepts obedience to that Empire's orders as necessary, or at least understandable, if we want to be assured of a 'good life', 'success', and 'security', the ultimate 'saving' benefits.

In short, we are dehumanised by our *selfishness,*[37]

and our *heartlessness* towards the dramatic facts of cruel poverty, AIDs, exclusion and discrimination. We are dehumanised by our *contempt* for poor and indigenous people, and for our mother Earth.

We regard this dehumanisation as quite natural and something we can do nothing about, because that is the way things are. We don't notice much since, unlike physical evils that lead to physical death, spiritual woes are not so easily reckoned. But they are extremely harmful.

The call to eliminate poverty is positive but the way in which it is carried out can be dehumanising, regardless of the results

The first dehumanising aspect of such attempts to eliminate poverty is the way human dignity is ignored, almost on principle, as if that dignity had nothing to do with the matter. Or accepting that any means of alleviating poverty will do. That way of thinking is not only unethical, but also dehumanising, because we are not talking about wild animals but human beings.

It is also dehumanising to accept so readily in practice, even if not in theory, the slow rate of progress in overcoming poverty and the targets countries set for themselves. From the viewpoint of abundance, the rate of progress may seem relatively human and quick, but from the viewpoint of poverty – and decency – it is inhumanly slow, and in some cases, as in some sub-Saharan countries, there has even been a postponement of the dates set. Development specialists have said that the Millennium Development Goals are flawed and will do little to diminish poverty.[38] 'Reducing by half the number of people suffering from hunger will take 145 years, and not be achieved by 2015, as 189 heads of state had guaranteed.'[39]

It is also dehumanising that in the search for solutions, ethics are sidelined. Abolishing hunger requires technological know-how and strategies and a good dose of political pragmatism. But ignoring ethics does matter. It matters for reasons of effectiveness: a top FAO official stated that 'solving the problem of hunger today is not basically an economic or political problem; it is an ethical problem.' And it matters on principle. If we can dispense with ethics to solve human problems, it means that efficiency and ethics can be divorced without damage to humanity. The ancient ideal, or at least aspiration, of marrying virtue and happiness vanishes. All that remains is pragmatism with its strong brutalising potential.

And the same can be said for the language which is often used about human problems like hunger: *political will* is needed. Firstly, that means recognising that the political will is just not there, since hunger continues. And secondly, since *political* will is merely *human* will, the language of politics is being used as a cover-up. If there is no political will, that simply means that there is no effective human will to eliminate hunger. Confronted with the scandal of a hungry world, the term 'political' will is less shaming. It is used because it is less blatant than 'human' will, which asks us straight out: do we human beings want to eliminate hunger? We can debate the politics of

this in order to seek a cop-out, and that is why the
term is preferred. There can be no cop-out when
we speak of the human will to eliminate hunger.

Let's leave it there. Jean Ziegler says: 'A child who
dies of hunger is murdered.'[40] Those words bring
Ivan Karamazov to mind.[41] Karamazov's anger
when children were torn apart by dogs by order of
a landlord, who was a former soldier, found no
consolation in the thought that those children
might go to a place where they would become at
one with a universal harmony. 'If they invite me to
that heaven, I'll refuse to go.'[42]

The ambiguous and evasive language of 'globalisation' is dehumanising

Language can dehumanise when it is used to
manipulate, conceal or deceive. So choosing to use
one kind of language or another is never an
unloaded choice. There is always a battle going on,
so that the language comes to mean what favours
certain interests, regardless of whether it corres-
ponds to the reality or not. This happens with
terms like 'democracy' and 'freedom'. It used to
happen with terms like 'socialism' and 'revolution'.
And it also happens with religious language,
beginning with the word 'God'. Whoever wins the
language battle has won half the war – and has
gained significant power.

I think something of the kind is happening
with the term *globalisation*. There is no doubt
that something new has happened in history, but
in order to express it, we don't use terms like
planetisation or a *more connected, interdependent*

humanity. The chosen term is globalisation and I don't think this has happened by chance. The use of this term suggests, at least subliminally, that 'something good' has happened, and of course globalisation sounds better and more human than capitalism. It suggests the idea of 'salvation', although many of its results are bad and sometimes perverse.

'Globalisation' implies a value judgement: *what is happening is good.* We are living in an *inclusive* world for all and it is – or soon will be – a substantially *homogeneous* and *harmonious* world for all. It is not that we are living in an irregular and misshapen polyhedron, although we could all fit into that too. We are living in a world on the road to *perfection.* That is what is explicitly suggested by the term globalisation: the beauty of *roundness* and the *equity* within the whole, the *equi*-distance between all points on the surface of the globe and its centre.[43] This globalised world is proclaimed as *eschatological* good news, what humanity has so long yearned for. Now it is proclaimed with better arguments – and greater hopes – than those put forward by Fukuyama with his 'end of history'. I'd like to respond with three criticisms.

Firstly, when we use the term globalisation today, we are failing to recognise that there have already been important kinds of globalisation in the past. I mention just two, which I heard about from Hinkelammert years ago. First, the European 'discovery' of America globalised our geography and broadened human self-understanding, especially with regard to the unity of the human race. In a very different way, the atomic bomb dropped on Hiroshima in 1945 also globalised the human species, in that case, through global fear: for the first time we saw the possibility of our whole species being wiped out. Both these events enabled us to see and value the global dimensions of the Earth and the human family. At the same time, they disclosed the ambiguity inherent in all creation. However, nowadays, our language does not take globalisation's ambiguity seriously: that it can be *either* planetisation *or* conquest,[44] it does not ask whether one of these aspects predominates, and which. Neither does our language express the fear that a globalised world can arouse, the powerlessness and sense of inevitability: the fear of being absorbed and losing cultural identity, fear of jobs being 'out-sourced' for the sake of higher profits, fear that new superpowers will arise …

My second criticism is of the assumption that globalisation automatically means progress. This is used as a way of justifying globalisation and promoting it. That is because the official West is not in the habit of assessing its past progress honestly, or of analysing critically what it considers to be progress today. However, a glance at the past will quickly disabuse that optimism. Jürgen Moltmann writes:

> The fields of history's corpses we have seen, make it impossible for us to have any ideology of progress or any taste for globalisation […] If the achievements of science and technology can be used for the annihilation of humanity (and if they can, some day they will be), it

becomes difficult to enthuse about the internet or genetic engineering.[45]

The anti-globalisation or 'alternative globalisation' movements do not want 'more progress' but 'another world'.

My third criticism is the strongest. It is that our language usually hides what gave rise to the term globalisation, and what continues to be most characteristic of it. The economist Luis de Sebastián calls globalisation 'the current situation of the world economy'.[46] It is 'real capitalism' today.[47] And clear-sightedly, he adds: 'Like any process of social change, globalisation has produced winners and losers, those who have done well out of it and victims.'[48]

Looking at the economic reality of globalisation, we learn two important things. Although it calls itself 'global', its *saving* power – its power to heal the world – is no different from other economic processes. It is not a matter of course that its results are all good. Globalisation also produces evils, losers, victims. And the way we assess it will depend on whether we are with the winners or the losers.

In a world of poverty, ostentatious abundance and silence in the face of wretched poverty are dehumanising, particularly because they happen both at once. Here are some recent examples.

Singapore, 6 July 2005. This was the ceremony at which the Olympic Committee revealed the result of the vote for London, the city that is to be the site of the 2012 Olympic Games, with their whole rhetoric of universality. However, the planetary aspect of the Games lacked any real awareness of the planet today, with all its various peoples and cultures. There was even less awareness of the oppression and domination of some by others, or of the wrongful ongoing wars. Reality was glossed over in the distorted, deceitful language of pomp.

Sport is celebrated as the human form at its nearest to being divine, but it is not really sport itself, but sport of the *elite*, which has sold its soul to commercialism. There are liturgical celebrations, Olympic Games, world championships, which look more and more like the Hollywood film world, or the fashion industry or *Hello!*. Its heart really lies on Wall Street. In view of the wretched poverty of sub-Saharan Africa, the money bandied about in European football or US basketball is disgusting.

The Singapore celebrations leave us with an image of pomp, waste and wealth-worship. They distract and titillate us, but above all they hypnotise us. They offer a symbolic screen-show of the whole planet, but without any concern for the six thousand million human beings who live on it – and the vast numbers who barely survive.

Gleneagles, Scotland, G8, 8 July 2005. On that day the powers-that-be posed, with a show of humility, as benefactors of humanity. They wrote off the debt of some African countries. But Aminata Traoré told them the truth: 'We are used to G8 declarations that are never put into effect ... Because of their free trade policies, what they will do is negotiate away the competitiveness of our economies in relation to the markets of the North.'[49]

The injustice is clear but we must stress how blatant it is. In seven world capitals the G8 promoted *Live 8* concerts as a campaign to develop awareness and solidarity, and raise funds for Africa. But in the end there was little real generosity. Critics allege that those who profited most from the concerts were their corporate sponsors, Time Warner, Ford Motor Company, Nokia, EMI Music, which benefited from increased sales and royalties once their initial sponsorship investments in the events had been recouped. Once again business won out over music and solidarity, and the North was enriched by Africa's pain.

Silence about the South goes hand in hand with such Northern boastfulness. One recent example: Médecins sans Frontières has just published a list of 'the most forgotten humanitarian crises in the international media during 2005'. They take for granted that there are countless crises going on, so they concentrate on 'the most painful and shameful', the 'humanitarian' crises. And since they also take for granted that crises tend to be forgotten, they focus on the 'most forgotten' ones. The Democratic Republic of Congo continues to head this list: 'Millions of people are suffering extreme want and daily violence, that has worsened over the last few months; nevertheless, they are completely ignored by the rest of the world.'[50] The reality of the Third World is silenced.

And as well as that, there is the ongoing forgetfulness, which has now become a matter of course. 9/11 is well known because it was a terrorist attack on the United States. But 10/7 is completely ignored. On 7 October 2001 the international democratic community bombed Afghanistan. The date 11 March 2004 is well known in Spain for the attack on Madrid. But on 20 March 2003 the bombing of Iraq began and nobody remembers that date. The poor have no calendar. They do not exist. Forgetting is natural. And all this happens in a world that is more connected than ever before, a *globalised* world.

The enormous gap between the rich and the poor is dehumanising

Lastly, the unfeeling acceptance of great wealth and great poverty existing side by side is dehumanising, even before we inquire whether there is any causal relationship between them. That inequality is now regarded as normal, as if it were a fact of nature rather than of history.

The parable of the rich man and Lazarus is the true image of our world. Apparently, the story originated in an Egyptian legend, taken up either by Jesus or Luke. That means that the scandal is age-old and has persisted throughout history. What strike me most strongly in the story are Abraham's final words to the rich man: 'They will not change even if someone rises from the dead' (Lk 16: 31). That is true. We don't know what needs to happen to make the 'international community' feel any remorse about this enormous inequality and respond to it with radical compassion.

All humanity should feel ashamed at this coexistence of the rich man and Lazarus, before even asking what has caused it. It is not merely unjust but disgraceful, that in a world of abundance, four hundred times more resources are spent on pregnancy care and the birth of a baby in the rich world than in Ethiopia; that a Salvadoran woman working in a sweat-shop should earn 29 cents for each shirt that the multinational Nike sells to the National Basketball Association (NBA) for 45 dollars; or that 'one kidnapped white person is more newsworthy than a thousand tortured and murdered Congolese';[51] that according to the UN Development Programme, the gap between rich and poor is rapidly widening – the disproportion of wealth has risen from 30 to 1 in 1960, to 60 to 1 in 1990 and 74 to 1 in 1997 – and more recent reports indicate that this trend is continuing.[52] And nobody cares. Eduardo Galeano says that: 'A US citizen is worth fifty Haitians.' And he wonders: 'What would happen if one Haitian were worth fifty US citizens?'

On 13 February 2001 a football game was played between Real Madrid and Lazio. The market value of the twenty-two players would have been 125 million pesetas (about 700 million dollars at that date). The sporting press[53] reported this before the game, not only without shame but with gloating satisfaction. But it didn't report that the figure was probably a high percentage of the national budget of a black African country, perhaps even twice the whole budget of Chad. And from what we hear, it doesn't sound as if things have changed much since then.

Let's leave it there. The wealth-civilisation gives

rise to many of these evils. Then it conceals them. It is a dehumanising civilisation. It makes the human spirit breathe poisoned air. Sometimes we hear strong words, like those we have quoted earlier. And there are other voices. John Paul II:

> More than ever today, the war of the powerful against the weak has created deep divisions between the rich and poor'.[54] (John Paul II)

> The richest, most powerful countries have abdicated from democratic principles (justice, freedom, equality, solidarity) in favour of the laws of the market.'[55] (Mayor Zaragoza)

> Unflinching, unswerving, fierce intellectual determination, as citizens, to define the real truth of our lives and our societies is a crucial obligation which devolves upon us all ... If such a determination is not embodied in our political vision, we have no hope of restoring what is so nearly lost to us – the dignity of man.[56] (Harold Pinter)

> We are debtors and we haven't got much time left to pay our debts.'[57] (J. Taubes)

And, hitting where it hurts their most cherished propaganda, what Ellacuría said about the United States remains true. The US mocks democracy and its principles. 'It does not respect humanity's majority will, or the sovereignty of other nations, or even UN resolutions passed by massive majority, or the judgements of The Hague International Court.'[58] Today he would denounce the barbarism of *preventive war* and its theoretical justification, and the atrocity of the term *collateral damage* for what they are: monstrous murders. All this continues to be relegated to silence and oblivion. The democracies do not treat it as a vital task to oppose such lies. And very few churches dare to take their prophetic duty seriously.

There will always be a Romero, a Casaldáliga, a Chomsky, a Galeano, as in the past we had Adorno and Martin Luther King. But they are not many. Nor do we have many like Ivan Karamazov, who are prepared to refuse to enter the heaven of this industrial, globalised, democratic world of ours, which produces – or tolerates – the deaths of children. And to express what is most dehumanising of all, we can adapt Bonhoeffer's phrase *etsi Deus non daretur* [even if there were no God] to *etsi pauperes darantur* [even though there are the poor]. What is most dehumanising of all is that, even though such terrible poverty exists, we can go on living normally in such a world.

3. THE POOR AND SALVATION

'Wretched man that I am! Who will deliver me from this body of death?' (Rom 7:24), Paul cried. We don't go in for that sort of question nowadays, but the horror aroused by the world we have described prompts a similar one: 'Who will deliver us from this cruel and inhuman world?'

As the problem is so enormous, our response can only be modest; at least, let's try to begin. We start by linking salvation to the poor, and by seeing the poor as the *setting* where salvation becomes possible. And although it sounds paradoxical, we begin with our modest formula *extra pauperes nulla salus* ('no salvation outside [or apart from] the poor'). Strictly speaking, we are not saying that with the poor salvation already exists automatically, but that without them it cannot exist at all. We *are* saying that there is always 'something' of salvation with the poor. What we want to do is offer hope, despite everything: *salvation for a very sick world can come from the world of the poor and the victims.*

Basically, we shall proceed by way of *mystagogy*, that is, by trying to enter into a mystery that is beyond us. We do not fully know what a human being is, so of course we do not fully know the meaning of salvation. Nevertheless, some of its elements are not at all mysterious, the abolition of hunger, for example. The formula *extra pauperes nulla salus* is also beyond us. Ideas and arguments are necessary to start penetrating the mystery, but they are not enough. We also need wisdom, reflection, witness and experience, and here we certainly also need what Pascal called *finesse*.

Our formula is a challenge to reason and hubris rebels against it. As far as I know, it does not appear, in any modern or postmodern texts, since it is not easy to accept that salvation can come from the unenlightened.[59] The prevalent metaphysical axiom is: 'saved or damned, it's us who are real.'

The formula only becomes meaningful when we analyse the various contributions of the poor to salvation. It is also a negative statement. That does not make it any less important, but rather more so. Indeed, it seems to me that the more important things are, the more they need to be formulated in negative terms.[60] But even with all these difficulties, we stand by the formula. It is a strong one and capable of breaking the logic of the wealth-civilisation – theoretically, at least.

The formula presents further difficulties. For some, the fundamental problem is the inability of the poor to produce goods on a large scale. For me, the major problem is that even within the world of the poor the *mysterium iniquitatis* also reigns. We think of the evils we see perpetrated daily there. Those who live and work among the poor constantly remind us. In one way or another, they ask us if we are not idealising the poor, or resorting to the 'myth of the noble savage', as I heard in Spain during the celebrations for the five hundredth anniversary of the arrival of Columbus in the Americas. It is not easy to give a satisfying answer. It is one thing to see the poor in their base communities, living generously, committed to liberation – their own and that of others – and inspired by someone like Archbishop Romero. It is another to see them fed up, ducking and diving for what a world of abundance has to offer, fighting one another to survive. Then there are also the horrors of the Great Lakes region of Africa which contains Rwanda, Burundi and the Democratic Republic of the Congo, or the dozen daily murders in El Salvador. All this happens among the poor, although the immediate responsibility for the horrors is not theirs alone, or always theirs at all. We do not think they bear the main responsibility. And we must also remember that their lives vary at different times and places.

Another difficulty is the theological novelty of the formula. There has always existed a relationship of some kind between the poor and Christian faith:

a) Faith moves us to strong indignation on behalf of the poor, boundless compassion and radical conversion, which can lead to an 'option for the poor' (Medellín) and to living in obedience to 'the authority of those who suffer' (J. B. Metz).
b) It can lead us to question whether and why we believe in God (theodicy), when it seems that God cannot or does not want to eliminate the horrors of our world.

c) Our salvation or condemnation depends on our attitude to the poor: 'Come, you blessed of my Father, because I was hungry and you gave me food. Depart from me, you cursed …' (Mt 25).

d) Finally, since we believers are 'sacraments' of God – displaying God's 'presence' or 'absence' – we can read the biblical denunciation one way or the other, depending on how we behave towards the poor. Five times (three referring to God and two to Christ) the Bible repeats: 'Because of you, God's name is despised among the nations' (Is 52:5 LXX version; Ez 36:20; Rom 2:24; James 2:7; 1 Peter 2:2). That might be us. Or, on the other hand, we can do what Jesus asks of us: 'Let your light so shine before men, that they may see your good works and give glory to your Father who is in heaven' (Mt 5:16).

Medellín accorded a special importance to the 'option for the poor'. But here we go one step further, take a new step. We are proposing the 'option to let salvation come from the poor'. That is not easy to accept and it requires a new logic. We are not just adding a bit more to an already established way of thinking. Our new logic derives from a fundamental attitude, which represents a breakthrough. We must not only be on the side of the poor and behave accordingly (Kant's question 'what must I *do?*') . But we must also ask Kant's two other questions: 'what can I *know?*' and 'what can I *hope?*' And we may add 'what can I *celebrate?*' and 'what can I *receive?*' And all this 'from the poor'. Since the poor become central in answering these questions, it means that our way of thinking is driven by a different logic. Then it becomes reasonable and understandable to accept our formula *extra pauperes nulla salus*. It is not easy, but nevertheless what this new logic *adds* is necessary.

That is what we are trying to offer in this brief essay. We are guided by Dom Pedro Casaldáliga's poetic, creative and prophetic intuition and by Ignacio Ellacuría's analytical intuition. The reader will be aware of the complexity and uncertainty with which our thinking must wrestle. We are encouraged to keep going by Rahner's 'It can't be like this', and also by some words of Dom Pedro Casaldáliga, who was kind enough to write to me: 'You are right to say, and we must keep repeating it: without [apart from] the poor there is no salvation, without [apart from] the poor there is no Church, without [apart from] the poor there is no gospel.' And of course, we hope that others will correct, improve and fill out what we are going to say.

Experiencing the new logic

People who come from the rich world to that of the poor and the victims often have the same experience: among the poor and the victims they find 'something' new and unexpected. They experience 'something' good and positive. They experience 'salvation'. José Comblin:

> The media always speak about the poor negatively, as those who do not possess goods, lack

culture, do not have enough to eat. Seen from the outside, the world of the poor is wholly negative. However, seen from within, the world of the poor has vitality, they struggle to survive, they invent 'informal' work, and build a different civilisation of solidarity, people who recognise each other as equals, with their own forms of expression, including their own art and poetry.[61]

This is saying that in the world of the poor there are important values, which constitute a civilisation of solidarity. And that is not just a single opinion; we find it repeatedly. Today many people are seeking a *humane* humanity – not a pleonasm – just as Luther sought a *kind* God. They do not find it in societies of abundance or in globalisation, or even in democratic society. But they do find important elements of it in the world of the poor: joy, creativity, patience, art and culture, hope, solidarity. It is a dialectical experience, since they have encountered human life on 'the far side of the rich world'. It is a saving experience because it arouses the hope of a more humane world. And it is an experience of grace because it rises from where it is least expected.

From Chile, Ronaldo Muñoz says something similar in response to the optimistic report of the 2005 UN Development Programme. He dampens the report's enthusiasm and reminds us of the serious evils that still afflict the majority. But above all he stresses the need to see things differently, from a different viewpoint:

We should rather be astonished by the

endurance, the personal and social development of the women: astonished at the spontaneous solidarity of so many poor people with their more needy neighbours; at the new adult and youth groups, who keep standing up against wind and tide to share their lives, work and celebrate together; amazed at the new dignity and protest struggle of the Mapuche people; the small Christian communities, both Catholic and Protestant, which continue to sprout up and bear fruits of fellowship and hope.[62]

From India Felix Wilfred describes what happened that was both positive and negative in the world of the poor during the Asian tsunami of 2004. He concludes:

Coping with human suffering and responding with compassion has developed in the victims some of the values we need for a different world: solidarity, humanity, a spirit of sharing, survival skills, risk-taking, dogged resistance to adversity. Unlike in the world of Empire and globalisation, in the world of the victims the good is not seen as mere 'success'. The good and the just are ideals the world needs in its struggle to attain something vital. The cultural resources of the poor reflect the values and ideals of a future world and help them to face life bravely, individually and together.[63]

The above words are remarkable and we leave it there. Obviously we cannot deduce a thesis from them, but what they say is crucial:

There is something that is found in the world of
the poor. The poor don't take life for granted (as
we who are not poor do), they die before their
time, they have (nearly) all the powers of the
world against them and still they have 'something' enabling them to live, 'something' they
offer us all. That 'something' does not consist
in material goods, but human goods. It has
humanising power. Those goods are not to be
found, or are found less easily, in the world of
those who are not poor.

The 'poor' suffering all the various forms of
poverty, as we analyse below, above all, the 'poor
with spirit' as Ellacuría calls them (thereby sys-
tematically linking the Luke and Matthew
Beatitudes),[64] are the ones who humanise and
offer salvation, the ones who can inspire and
encourage us to create a civilisation of solidarity,
rather than selfishness. That is why Ellacuría spoke
of 'the enormous spiritual and human wealth of
the poor and the peoples of the Third World.'[65]
How many poor people like that there really are
will vary at different times and places. Of course,
not all the poor are like that. In their world
goodness and evil frequently exist side by side,
especially in times of crisis. But for the healing of a
very sick society, I believe there are more than
enough of them. The problem is taking any notice
of them.

Most important of all, in the world of the poor a
new logic is generated, which allows reality to be
seen in a different way. It enables people to see
that salvation cannot just be identified with

progress and development. We consider this to be very important. And it makes us see that salvation can come from the poor. For us who are not poor, it is an experience of grace. The option for the poor is not just a matter of *giving* to them, but of *receiving* from them.

The logic of salvation in the biblical-Christian tradition

What we have just said should not come as a total surprise, although it needs careful explaining. The nucleus of its logic is already present – in idealised form – in the biblical Jesus tradition, even though western culture chooses to ignore it. What makes for salvation in its various dimensions is fully symbolised in that tradition. In its historical and social dimension it appears as the *kingdom of God*; in the personal, as *heart of flesh;* transcendently, as a *new heaven.* We should not seek for salvation models or recipes here, but we can find fundamental concepts about how salvation comes and the way it is expressed.

It is essential to that tradition that *salvation comes from the world of the poor* and unfolds outwards from there. The Old Testament makes plain Yahweh's preference for a poor, oppressed people. Furthermore, it is made clear at important moments that the symbolic bearers of salvation are the poor and weak and, above all – mysteriously – the victims, the servant in his individual and collective dimension. Conversely, salvation does not come from above, from the realm of power and abundance. In fact, in the Deuteronomic tradition the kings – symbols of power – do not show up at all well, with only two exceptions, Josiah and Hezekiah.

Jesus is also presented from that viewpoint, as is the salvation he brings. The story of Jesus himself, the saviour, insists on his littleness: 'we know where he comes from' (Jn 6:41), from Nazareth, a small, remote village out of which nothing good can come. Transcendentally, we are told that he became *sarx*, flesh with all its weaknesses (Jn 1:14). But I want to stress something which is often overlooked. I wonder whence salvation, in its historical form, came to Jesus, and whether something of it also came from the world of the poor. I don't know whether or how much we can gather about this from the gospels, but I think the matter is crucial. And the question should not shock us, because it is also said about Jesus, for example, that he stood before God with joy and doubts. As the letter to the Hebrews says, he was like us in *everything* except sin (Heb 4:15). He was the first born, the elder brother in faith (Heb 12:2).

That is why we can ask if there are any indications as to whether Jesus was not only salvation for others himself; but whether – as well as his Father in heaven – others, the poor of the Earth, were salvation and good news for him. We can find a hint of this in his words: 'I thank you, Father, that you have hidden these things from the wise and prudent and revealed them to the little people' (Mt 11:25). Was Jesus just full of joy or did he feel that he himself was being evangelised by those little people?

We may wonder what Jesus felt about the faith of the little people when he said to the woman with the flow of blood and to blind Bartimaeus (Mk 5:34; 10:52): 'Your faith has healed you,' and to the sinful woman in the house of Simon the Pharisee: 'Go in peace, your faith has saved you' (Lk 7:50); or when he saw a poor widow contributing a few pence in the temple, giving more than all the others, because she was giving everything she had to live on (Mk 12:44). Or the Canaanite woman, who told Jesus he was right: 'Yes, Lord.' But then in her moving way she goes on to correct him: 'Yet even the dogs eat the crumbs that fall from their master's table.' And Jesus responded: 'Great is your faith' (Mt 15:28). Without stretching our imagination, we may well wonder whether Jesus felt *grateful* for the faith of these simple people, whether he said to himself, like Archbishop Romero: 'With these people it's not hard to be a good shepherd.' That is to say, did Jesus himself experience salvation coming from the poor?

The most important thing in understanding the logic of salvation in that biblical-Jesus tradition is its theological foundation. In order to become a God of salvation *the Most High came down* into our history and he did so in two ways: he came down into the human, and within the human, he came down to what is humanly weak. To put it succinctly, *transcendence* has become *transdescent:* intimate kindness, and *condescension:* warm welcome. And the same thing was said in the christological language of the early centuries: *salus autem quoniam caro.* Christ is salvation because he is flesh, *caro* (Latin), *sarx* (Greek). That is the new logic.

In principle, it is easy to grasp this logic any-where. But it does not usually happen outside the world of the poor. In corroboration, I'd like to quote some Jesuits of the Third World – I'll explain why later. They are well aware of the complexity of salvation. They speak about it in different contexts. But they all share the same fundamental insight.

From Sri Lanka, Aloysius Pieris writes that the poor are chosen for a saving mission, not because they are saints, but because they are the powerless, the rejected: 'They are called to be mediators of salvation for the rich, and the weak are called to liberate the strong.'[66] Engelbert Mveng speaks from the context of Cameroon: 'The Church of Africa [...] must announce the good news of liberation to those who have succumbed to the temptation of power, wealth and domination.'[67] From El Salvador we have already seen Ignacio Ellacuría's proposal: the poverty-civilisation is necessary to overcome and redeem the evils generated by the wealth-civilisation.[68] And from Venezuela Pedro Trigo writes:

> As against the dominant view that maintains that the salvation of (some of) the poor can only happen as a spill-over or by-product of the health of the [economic] system, Jesus' mission (and hence the Christian mission) proclaims that the salvation of the non-poor will happen as a sharing in the salvation of the poor. Nowadays this sounds like non-sense.[69]

The reason for quoting Jesuits in this context is that they may well be influenced by the meditation on the two flags in St Ignatius' *Spiritual Exercises* (nn.136-148). The meditation presents two opposite dynamic 'reality principles'. One of them leads to humility and thus to all the virtues; the other leads to pride and thus to all the vices; or in our terms, one of them leads to salvation, and the other to condemnation. St Ignatius also stresses that what each principle generates, at each step of the process, stands in a dialectical relationship with what is generated by its opposite: insults as opposed to worldly honours; humility as opposed to pride; all the virtues as opposed to all the vices. The important thing is to grasp what lies at the root of it all: *poverty*, which leads to all the virtues, to salvation; as opposed to wealth, which leads to all the vices, to condemnation. That insight does not have to be confined to the individual way of perfection; it can also apply to history. Ellacuría thinks that 'it is to do with arousing energies that can shape a new world.'[70] Starting from the (civilisation of) poverty as against the (civilisation of) wealth, we can change this world.

We have already said that this thesis is *counter-cultural*, as it was in Bonhoeffer's day: 'only a suffering God can save us'. It is also *defenceless*, because the world of the poor is pervaded by non-salvation, the *mysterium iniquitatis*. And the biblical basis to support it – 'the suffering servant brings salvation' – is a great affront to reason. But it is *necessary*. Left to itself the world of abundance does not save, it does not produce life for all and it does not make for humanity.

What salvation and what poor?

We have argued that in the world of the poor there is a saving 'something', which is not easily found in other worlds. We'll say more about this shortly. But first we must be clear what we mean by 'salvation' and what we mean by 'poor'.

Kinds of salvation

Human salvation and the need for it operate in different spheres. There is *personal* salvation and *social* salvation; there is *historical* salvation and *transcendent* salvation, although they cannot always be clearly separated. Here we shall concentrate on the historical and social salvation of a society that is very sick. We must also distinguish between salvation as *a positive state of affairs* and as the *process* of getting there. In both cases salvation is dialectic, and sometimes produces a conflict. It occurs in opposition to other realities and processes, and may involve a struggle against them.

As a state of affairs salvation occurs in different forms. Taking the lack of life and dehumanisation we have been talking about *sub specie contrarii,* we can say the following: salvation is *life* (satisfaction of basic needs), as against poverty, illness and death; it is *dignity* (respect for persons and their rights), as against heedlessness and contempt; it is *freedom* as against oppression; salvation is *fellowship* among human beings, brought together as a *family,* as against the Darwinian view that regards humanity as a mere *species;* salvation is *fresh air,* which the spirit can breathe in its movement towards the human (honesty, compassion, solidarity, openness to some form of transcendence), as against what is dehumanising (selfishness, cruelty, individualism, arrogance, blunt positivism).

Salvation is concrete – as we see in the various kinds of salvation in the synoptic gospels. We must remember this so that we do not try unhistorically to 'universalise' the idea of salvation and the positive or negative concepts that go with it, such as *poverty* and *development*, for example. That is what the UN Development Programme does. It has its advantages, but of course, whether it actually is salvation will be understood differently in the residential districts of Paris and World Bank reports, or in the refugee camps in the Great Lakes region of Africa and the experiences of grassroots communities. From Brazil Dom Pedro Casaldáliga wrote that 'freedom without justice is like a flower on a corpse'. 'Freedom' and 'justice' are both expressions of salvation, but we must not assume that we can understand them adequately from some supposedly universal standpoint, or thence prioritise how they are needed or how urgently.

This raises the question of the *setting* in which to think about salvation. That is an important task today, because the ideology of globalisation tries to make us believe that the world's reality is substantially homogeneous, and therefore it is unnecessary to seek the 'most adequate' setting in which to discover what salvation is; or to ask what it means to be human, or what hope means, or sin, or God. Liberation theology does not operate in that way. It regards it as extremely important to

determine the adequate setting in which to discover how things really are. That setting is the
world of the poor. That is why liberation theology, unlike any other, has been able to formulate,
albeit negatively, the setting of theology as *extra
pauperes nulla salus.*

Lastly, we must also take into account the
various forms taken by the *process* of salvation. It
normally occurs in opposition to structures of
oppression; hence salvation takes the form of
liberation: the need to be freed from ... Moreover,
there is often the need not only to struggle against
negative factors generated by such structures, but
also to eradicate them; thus salvation becomes
redemption. And according to the biblical-
Christian tradition, in order for this to happen, we
have to take responsibility for sin. Therefore of its
nature, redemption is a struggle against evil, not
only from outside, but also *within*: we have to
shoulder the responsibility for it.

Various aspects of the lives of the poor

We also need to determine the various aspects of
being poor, because the way a life of poverty is led
will affect its contribution to salvation.[71]

Before going into more detail, it is important to
remind ourselves of the fundamental distinction
made at the 1979 Conference of the Bishops of
Latin America at Puebla in its approach to the
salvation offered by the poor. Firstly, *just by what
they are* and independently of 'their personal or
moral situation',[72] the poor 'constantly challenge
[the Church], calling her to conversion', and such

calling to conversion is very valuable. Secondly, the poor *evangelise* and save, 'since many of them practise in their lives the gospel values of solidarity, service, simplicity and readiness to receive God's gift' (n.1147). That is the spirit in which they live their lives. Let us see who those poor people are.

Firstly, there are the *materially* poor, those who do not take life for granted, those for whom just staying alive is their main concern, those who live on familiar terms with death, or some sort of death – of their dignity or their culture. This is the *economic* state of being poor, in the basic sense: their *oikos,* minimal life support system, is threatened. The poor are those who 'die before their time'.

Secondly, there are the *dialectically* poor. They are not poor because nature does not yield them enough, but because they have been impoverished and oppressed. They are deprived of the fruits of their labour and, increasingly, they are deprived of work itself. Likewise they are deprived of social and political power by those who have enriched themselves by plunder, and taken power. That is the *sociological* meaning of being poor: they are denied as 'social' beings, excluded from fellowship. Moreover, as a general rule they are scorned and ignored. They have no name either in life or in death, as if they didn't exist.

Thirdly, there are the *consciously* poor, those who have become aware, individually and collectively, of the fact of material poverty and its causes. They have awoken from the dogmatic dream with which they had been conned: that their poverty is natural and inevitable – sometimes, even the will of God.

Fourthly, there are the *freedom-seeking* poor,

those who convert their awareness into grassroots organisation and work in solidarity to liberate themselves. They have become aware of what they can do and of their responsibility towards *all* the poor. They emerge from their own groups and communities to set others free.

Fifthly, there are the spiritually poor. By spirituality we mean something precise here: those who live their material lives with awareness and give freely, with hope and kindness. Steadfast under persecution, they act with love, even that greatest love, which is giving your life for the liberation of the poor masses (that is, living the spirit of the Beatitudes). And they live that way with confidence in a Father-God, a Father in whom they can trust and rest. At the same time they are available to do his will, as he does not let them rest (like the spirit of Jesus before the mystery of God). Those are the poor *with spirit.*

Lastly, if we consider the poor from the viewpoint of Christian faith, their poverty has a *theological* dimension: God prefers them; and a *christological* dimension: Christ's presence in them. So – at least to the extent that believers see Christ's presence in them – that radicalises both what the poor can demand from the non-poor, and what they can offer them.

The various aspects of the life of the poor – according to times and places – will produce different fruits of salvation. Briefly, their harsh lives can give rise to conversion and compassion, and also to truth and action for justice. And by their spirit the poor can humanise in various ways the impure air *our* spirits breathe.

Historical forms of salvation coming from the world of the poor

It is not easy to describe the salvation that comes from the world of the poor. It may help to think of it in three forms: as a way of overcoming de-humanisation; as positive humanising factors for accomplishing good things; and as an invitation to universal solidarity.

Overcoming dehumanisation

As we have already said, by what they are, the poor can motivate others to be converted. If they can't, who can? Perhaps this is the main emphasis in our saying *'extra' pauperes:* outside, apart from the poor there is no easy way of being converted. The non-poor can see the huge sufferings of the poor and the world's cruelty towards them. They can compare their own comfortable life with the lives of the poor, especially if they have come to think of their own life as a manifest destiny, and can recog-nise their sin. None of that is easy and it does not happen all the time, but the offer is always there.

Society may boast that it has got over ideas like *conversion,* but that is a grave mistake. Other concepts such as change, wanting a different world, do not express how radical the need is for a new direction and way of behaving. Even less do they convey the pain involved, the repentance and firm purpose of amendment, all that is implied in conversion. And positively, conversion can lead to truth, hope and action. In it human beings can find answers to their most fundamental questions.

What can I know?

The poor are *bearers of truth*. By what they are, they enlighten the world of abundance so that it can see its truth and thus proceed to the *whole* truth. Ellacuría explained this in two vigorous metaphors. First, the crucified people are like a mirror in which the First World sees itself the other way round, and recognises the truth about itself that otherwise, by every possible means, it tries to hide. Second, the reality of the crucified peoples is also revealed by 'coproanalysis': the faeces show what the First World produces, and thus reveal its true state of health.[73]

Even if it is uncomfortable, it is foolish to scorn that light. Science analyses reality, but to see it as it is, first and foremost, what is needed is light. The light that comes from the poor can dispel our wilful blindness.[74] It can wake us up from the dream in which the West is sunk: the dream of its own reality. That is how Ellacuría saw things, and that is what he said about the Central American University: At least it tries to 'work in the light, the light that the oppressed masses of the world shed upon the world, by which some are blinded but others are enlightened.'[75]

What can I hope for?

The poor deliver the rebirth of *utopia*, the vision of which was valued so highly in the time of Bloch but has been so downgraded nowadays by post-modernity. Moreover, the poor have a very clear idea of it. Utopia is a life of dignity and justice for the poor masses, not an ideal life – impossible – of social and political perfection, conceived out of abundance, as in Plato's *Republic* or Thomas More or Campanella (with, respectively, their naturalistic, theocratic and aristocratically communist utopias).

The poor change the very meaning of historical utopia, and that is their most important contribution: it does not mean *ou-topia*: nowhere, but *eu-topia*: the good place, what has got to take place. What we call the 'good life', 'quality of life', 'welfare state' – prosperity for the minorities – are milestones along to the road towards a utopia conceived out of the abundance of the non-poor. But of course, the non-poor are not content to leave it there. They go on to set up a frantic race for 'progress' – dashing ahead despite the fact that humanity as a whole is in crisis. In contrast, the *oikos*, the existence and guarantee of a minimal core of life for the human family is the utopia of the poor.

And at the same time, from the poor comes hope, *real* hope, meaning what we should really hope for. In the 'world of abundance' there are expectations, arising from calculations, but there is no radical break between the present and the future. All very well, but it is not hope, because in Christian terms, hope means hoping against hope. The ground of hope does not lie in objective calculation, or in subjective optimism. It lies in love, that shoulders everything. The hope of the poor undergoes crises, periods of impatient disappointment, because measurable immediate results and

victories do not appear.[76] But there is a faith that
overcomes darkness and a hope that triumphs
over disappointment, as is shown in the historical
patience of the poor and their determination to
live. That is what we call essential holiness. That
hope is what they offer the First World. Comparing
the First World to the hope that he saw in Latin
America, Ellacuría used to say: 'The only thing
they really have is fear.'[77]

What must I do?

The poor set out what must be done and the road
action must take. Here we note two points, both
very necessary today. First, as well as telling and
demanding the truth, the poor make it possible to
speak out truly and prophetically. Fundamentally,
they show that it is vital to speak out in order to
accord with reality, that is, to be *real*. So it is a serious mistake to minimise the need for prophecy
and dismiss it as mere protest. We have to go
beyond psychology. Prophetic outspokenness has
got to echo a reality that needs expressing.
Speaking out is 'voicing an oppressed reality that
has been made voiceless'. If mere protest were an
easy matter, as is sometimes simplistically or
cynically supposed, speaking out prophetically is
not. It is costly, because in order to echo the reality
you have to *be in it* (incarnation), *see it* as it is
(honesty), and above all you have to *be moved* to
compassion and decide to work for justice
(shouldering the reality), accepting the
consequences of persecution or even death that
this may involve (bearing the reality).[78]

Secondly, because poverty is intolerable, we need the energy not just to speak out against it, but to create economic, political and cultural models to overcome it, as Ellacuría also said. Here it is true that there is 'no protest without a proposal'. And in any case the poor demand that the new models should not be inhuman or dehumanising.

Signs and yeast

Personally and communally, the poor have remarkable values, which are generally ignored: resistance, simplicity, joy in life's fundamentals, welcome for God's mystery etc, as we saw in what José Comblín, Ronaldo Muñoz and Felix Wilfred said. With those values they create social forms, though these may look modest to outsiders. I think these values are above all *humanising*. They are important for living in a more human way, but they also make it possible to produce things of fundamental value.

The poor offer models, which are sometimes slight, sometimes remarkable – but *their own* – of grassroots economics, community organisation, health, housing, human rights, education, culture, religion, politics, art, sport ... In many cultures they have a deep ecological awareness and take better care of nature and Mother Earth than the West does.

And, depending on where they are and their situation, the poor organise themselves into liberation movements, which may even be revolutionary. They gather social and/or political strength, depending on the issues. They do this to defend their rights, but also the rights of other poor and oppressed people – sometimes the rights of a whole community. They seek and sometimes gain power. This may lay them open to the danger of dehumanisation, but they often show great generosity, which keeps them human. And they get results.

Put simply, the poor have values and produce positive results, which, though they may not represent massive changes to social forms, do point the way and do offer elements of a new society. Sometimes they do not stay within their own communities, but appear as a *sign* for others. Like the light in the gospel, they shine forth and light up their surroundings. Then they can become like *yeast*, which makes the dough rise, and *salt*, which makes it tasty. That is to say they produce *salvation* beyond themselves. Ellacuría saw this in grassroots communities and, specifically in the base communities:

> There are signs that the poor are gospel-bringers, saviours. The marvellous experience of the base communities as a ferment of Church renewal and as a factor in political transformation, and the quite common example of 'poor with spirit', who organise struggle in solidarity and risk martyrdom for the sake of their brothers and sisters, for the weakest and humblest, are proof of the saving, liberating power of the poor.[79]

Calling the human family to solidarity

The poor give rise to solidarity. Solidarity, as it has been beautifully called, is 'the tenderness of peoples'. We have defined it as 'those who are unequal carrying each other'. But we need to analyse the idea fully and look at what the poor contribute. Solidarity means the poor and the non-poor carrying each other, giving to one another and receiving from one another the best we have, so as to become 'with one another'.[80] Often what is given and what is received are things of a different kind: material help and human welcome, for example. And what the non-poor receive may be more, in human terms, than what they give. This sort of solidarity goes beyond mere one-way aid, with its inbuilt tendency to impose and dominate. And it also goes beyond an alliance between people wanting to defend their own common interest against others.

Understanding solidarity as those who are unequal carrying each other is something new. But in an unequal world it is necessary. Solidarity can radically resolve the ambiguity, and right what is wrong in the falsely universalising concept of globalisation. But what is most important is that the call to solidarity of this kind, should not come from just anywhere, but from the poor. Historically, it happens locally, in small ways, in Nicaragua or El Salvador, but it is an enormous contribution to our understanding of solidarity, especially now with the proliferation of aid organisations and ideologies, both private and governmental, religious and secular. I think it is vital that their actions should be imbued with the energy of carrying one another, and not according to the largely self-interested directives of the United Nations, European Community ...

Victims and Redemption

Historically, the poor are *victims,* and as such they also shape the liberation process, now in the form of redemption. Without aiming at theological precision, Archbishop Romero said with clear insight: 'Christ wanted to set his redemption seat among the poor' (Homily of 24 December 1978).

Today the term *redemption* is ignored, as if it had nothing important to say about healing a sick world. But it does. In the salvation process, there are many evils to eliminate, and a *struggle* to be engaged in against the structures which produce them. But when the evil is deep, lasting and structural, real healing means *eradicating* it. That task is so difficult that people have always been aware that it requires extraordinary strength, above the normal. In metaphorical language, this was expressed by saying that to heal a sinful world, there was 'a price to pay', which is the etymological meaning of the word redemption, *redemptio.* In other words, something hard had to be 'added' to the normal work and suffering required to produce good. In more historical language, we may say that in order to eradicate evil, we have to fight against it, not only from the outside, but from within. We have to be prepared to let the evil grind us down. Here we have the 'extra' suffering that always goes with redemption in history.

We have often said this in El Salvador in the face of violence. Violence has to be fought in various ways: from the outside, with ideas, negotiations and in extreme cases, tragically, even with more violence. That counter-violence should take the most humane form possible. But to redeem violence, it also has to be fought from within, that is, we must be ready to take it upon our shoulders. Martyrs for justice such as Gandhi, Martin Luther King and Archbishop Romero bear witness to this. That is what Ignacio Ellacuría said, as if by premonition, on 19 September 1989, two months before he himself fell victim to that violence. Indeed the speech he made in the presence of Presidents Oscar Arías of Costa Rica and Alfredo Cristiani of El Salvador in an attempt to carry forward peace negotiations was openly political and did not sound religious at all:

> There has been enormous pain and much bloodshed, but the classical theological maxim *nulla redemptio sine efusione sanguinis* reminds us that the salvation and liberation of peoples entails very painful sacrifices.[81]

We have to understand that saying properly. We are not defending Anselm's theory, of suffering as necessary – and effective – to appease the wrath of God and thus attain salvation.[82] In order to save us, God does not demand a sacrifice that kills his creatures, so there is no need to seek for excellence in the sacrificial victims. Nevertheless, by their suffering the victims can 'disarm' the power of evil, not magically but historically. That is a way of trying to explain the idea of what is saving in Christ's sufferings on the cross: sin has unleashed all its strength against him, but in so doing, sin itself loses its own strength. Therefore it is not that the suffering *appeases God* and wins his good will, but that it *disarms evil.* God accepts us precisely at the moment when he might have rejected us, because of the suffering we have inflicted on his Son. Thus the cross becomes a proof of his love.

Neither are we defending any sort of cult of sacrifice, as if suffering in itself were good for human beings. We do say that we should reverence the victims who suffer because they present much of the *mysterium tremendum et fascinans.* We should also be grateful to them, because their suffering often goes with, or results from, great generosity and even greater love. We reverence and give thanks for something fundamentally positive: in this cruel world, and against this cruel world, true love has appeared.

Redemption continues to be *mysterium magnum,* but sometimes a miracle happens and the mystery appears visibly as *mysterium salutis.* We can only speak of this with fear and trembling. Above all, we should only speak of it when we have decided to give life to the victims and commit our own lives to doing so. But out of respect for the victims and for our own sakes too, we should not ignore their saving power: we should not impoverish ourselves even more. As we have already described, innocent victims save by moving us to conversion, impelling us to honesty, hope and

active solidarity. And sometimes even in the midst
of such horrors they produce immediate and
tangible fruits of salvation, like a yeast of humanity permeating our common dough. That is the
miracle of redemption offered and received.

> In Auschwitz prisoner denies prisoner, but
> Father Kolbe broke that rule: now a prisoner
> offers his life for another prisoner, for some-
> one he does not know [...] Although the
> enlightenment – so rationalist and reasonable
> – does not get it, even in Auschwitz it is possi-
> ble to live with loving grace and in conversa-
> tion with the light ... [...] to arouse hope and
> prevent the despair of the other condemned
> prisoners. [83]

'We can go on praying after Auschwitz because
they went on praying in Auschwitz,'[84] as J. B. Metz
succinctly puts it, not a theologian given to easy
theodicy. And Etty Hillesum wrote that in
Auschwitz she felt she had to 'help God as much as
possible.'[85] Suffering brought about redemption.

The Great Lakes region of Africa is the Auschwitz
of today. There too we have seen incredible
humanity.

> It is not difficult to sing praises when every-
> thing is all right. The wonder is that [...] when
> the prisoners in Kigali today receive visits
> from their families, who bring them some-
> thing to eat with the greatest difficulty, they
> bless and give thanks to God. How can they
> fail to be his favourites! And how can we fail to
> learn gratitude from them. Today I received a

letter from them. Perhaps they do not realise how much we receive from them and how they save us.[86]

When the peace agreements were signed in El Salvador in 1992, the part played by the martyrs and the fallen in reaching them was strongly emphasised. Though they are often bandied about, these words contain a profound truth. And as in Auschwitz and the Great Lakes, the 'extra' suffering generated redemption, and the offer of humanisation. In a Salvadoran wartime refugee camp, on the Day of the Dead, the peasants prayed for their family members who had been murdered, and also for their murderers. They said: 'You know, we believe that our enemies should be on the altar too. Even though they kill us and murder us, they are our brothers. You know the Bible tells us: it's easy to love our own, but God also asks us to love those who persecute us.'[87] We don't know whether the killers ever received that offer of salvation made by their victims, or whether they accepted it. But the victims' prayer for their killers and other loving actions steeped the world in humanity. Such capital should not be squandered but invested like a great treasure.

That treasure is grace. And those who ask what is the point of mentioning it in speaking of a sick society, have not understood Jesus of Nazareth, or human beings, or the society in which we live, full of sin but also shot through by the grace of these victims. We become human not only by our own self-making, which is often a Promethean under-taking, but also by letting ourselves be made human by other people. Salvation lies in that gift.

The times do not seem to be right for talking like that. Our society's – understandable but dangerous – goal is to save *only* by producing goods, as if then its evils would disappear of their own accord, without leaving any scars and without sin's habit of 'creeping back', to produce death and inhumanity *again*. Therefore it is not possible to speak about redemption without bearing in mind the historical need for it.

That appears very clearly when we analyse what the martyrs of our time provide.[88] The Jesuanic martyrs are those who live and die like Jesus, whom we call active martyrs. Those who are slowly killed by unjust poverty and/or violently in massacres are the anonymous martyrs. Taken as a whole, these Jesuanic martyrs are the great redemption-bringers today. And strictly speaking, the latter are more so than the former, even though there is often no clear dividing line between them. They shoulder the sin of the world and weaken the roots of evil – even though they never manage to eradicate them completely. That is how they bring salvation.

Faith is needed to see things that way, as in the case of Yahweh's suffering servant. But sometimes it is plain to see. The case of Archbishop Romero is paradigmatic. A bishop, persecuted by all kinds of local powers, murdered, innocent and defenceless as he was, by mercenaries with the connivance of Empire, produced hope, fostered commitment and unprecedented universal solidarity.[89] Archbishop Romero was not just an individual but, I think we can say, he was the most visible head of a whole people, who fought against the sin of the world and took it upon their own shoulders.

Without trivialising the problem of theodicy, on the one hand, and without falling for a victim cult, on the other, we believe that the enormous suffering of the victims has 'something' that can heal our world. Iván Karamazov was right to refuse entry into a heaven where people had to go to restore a lost harmony. But we *do* accept entry into a world destroyed, which we have to go down into in order to come across that 'something' of humanity. Seeking suffering in order to find salvation would be blasphemy. [90] But in the face of of the victims' suffering, it is arrogant not to acknowledge its saving power and allow them to welcome us.

Redemption is necessary. 'linking the future of humanity to the fate of the poor has become a historical necessity [...] only the victims can redeem it.'[91] And it can be done, just as Christ on the cross, also in history, can unite suffering and total love. And then love saves. As Nelly Sachs says, 'They loved so much that they made night's granite jump about and smash to pieces.'[92]

The analogy of being 'in the world of the poor'

So what salvation can arise in the world of the non-poor? Of course, they can co-operate in healing a very sick world, but only on one condition: that they share really and historically, not just spiritually with good intentions, in the world of the poor.

Valuable things are generated among the non-poor: the science of Pasteur and Einstein, the revolution of liberty, equality and fraternity, the universal declarations of human rights, economic models which can overcome hunger, and the political power to implement them. And this is also true of the globalisation we have criticised.[93] That goes without saying.

The non-poor may also be necessary to foster the salvation that comes from the poor. They can become prophetic figures, so that the poor can recover and keep their self-confidence, develop action and inspire hope. When such figures do not appear, the poor may feel frustration, whereas when they do, the community becomes empowered and stirred. Those figures may arise from among the poor themselves, but also from among the non-poor. Archbishop Romero and University Rector Ellacuría did not come from the world of the poor. But by going down into it, they themselves received salvation, and the poor were empowered as saviours.

However, left to itself, there is no evidence that the world of abundance can bring salvation, and normally what it brings is ambiguous: Hiroshima or useful energy; food and health or individualist consumerism and soulless commodification; universalisation or conquest. And it is usually intermingled with sinfulness: domination, violence – as well as the arrogance of posing as a benefactor. For salvation to come from this world, it is not enough for it merely to produce valuable things, and pile them up upon its evils, but it must also purify its ambiguity and heal its sinfulness.

Of course the world of the non-poor has the potential to do both those things: offering general ethical, humanist and religious proposals. But the most radical possibility, without which no others usually suffice, is to go down into the poor in history.

That does not often happen on our own initiative, only when we are invited or impelled, by the poor themselves. It's difficult but it can happen, and in various ways. It is a matter of sharing in some way, *analogically* but *really*, the real world of the poor.

It can happen by actually *entering* that world and working on its behalf. It can happen by liberating action side by side with the poor, in the risks you take to defend them, by sharing their fate of persecution and death, by coming to share in their joys and hopes, by really doing things, not just having good intentions. And when there is this real sharing, however analogous it may be, then salvation can come from the world of abundance too. But we must be clear that it does *not* include the analogy of mere good intentions, which does not get its hands dirty with real poverty. Some people think that sharing in that world today is not necessary, because to bring about salvation all that is needed is well-managed self-interest, without having to pay any significant price. That is what our times have to suggest: neither generosity nor sacrifice are needed for salvation. Remember the old lie: being 'poor in spirit' without any kind of sharing in real poverty.[94]

4. EXTRA PAUPERES NULLA SALUS

We could have written all the above without mentioning our formula *extra pauperes nulla salus.* Moreover that formula does not appear either in traditional or progressive theology, or even as a formula in liberation theology, although it is in accord with it. We use it because as a formula it has theological roots which go back to Origen and Cyprian's *extra ecclesiam nulla salus,* and because it is a radical statement of the problem of salvation's setting.

After Vatican II, Schillebeeckx wrote: *extra mundum nulla salus* ('outside the world there is no salvation'), rephrasing the traditional formula. By that he meant that 'the world and human history in which God wants to bring about salvation, are the foundations of faith's whole reality; we are saved or lost, first and foremost, in the world. In that sense, *extra mundum nulla salus* is true.' [95] By that definition of salvation's *setting* Schillebeeckx made good use of the Council's radical break – its *globalising caesura.*[96] That new formula avoids the rigorist interpretation's danger of exclusivism: not just the Church but also the world is the setting for salvation.[97] It also avoids the danger of reductionism: salvation is not only religious, but it also has a historical and social dimension.[98]

That *caesura* or break was an epoch-making novelty, only comparable with what was decided at the Council – or rather, assembly – of Jerusalem: salvation is possible for all human beings, without their having to become Jews. That put an end to Jewish religious exclusiveness. Rahner was right to say that Vatican II was the most important council in the Church's history since the Council of Jerusalem.

However, shortly afterwards, at Medellín another even greater break or *caesura* occurred, which also affected our understanding of salvation and its setting. Medellín was a result of the Second Vatican Council, one of its most important ones, perhaps even *the* most important.[99] It went further than the Council by relating faith and the Church not to the *world*, but to the *poor.* And it did the same with theology. In its intellectual work it gave hermeneutical privilege to the poor, that is, it put them first in its efforts to understand texts and realities – that is what liberation theology did. All the *content* of theology was to be seen in relation to the poor. Thus Medellín proclaimed 'the Church of the poor'. The Council had not got very far with this, despite the fruitless efforts of John XXIII, Cardinal Lercaro and Bishop Himmer of Tournai with their formula *primus locus in Ecclesia pauperibus reservandus est* ('the poor are reserved the first place in the church'). Then at a crowning moment for theology, Archbishop Romero reformulated Irenaeus' phrase as *gloria Dei vivens pauper.*[100] He reformulated God's mystery in terms of the poor. I think that we still haven't grasped the boldness and novelty of this idea; we tend to treat his words as beautiful rhetoric. Theology also made a radical search for the *setting* in which to find God. Porfirio Miranda answered: 'The question is not whether someone is seeking God or not, but whether they are seeking him where he himself said he was to be found',[101] among the poor of this world.

From that dynamic of 'among the poor', new thinking arose about the setting in which salvation is to be found. Thus we arrived at the formula *extra pauperes nulla salus*: outside [apart from] the poor there is no salvation. I read it first in Javier Vitoria's doctoral thesis on Christian salvation from the viewpoint of liberation theology.[102] Then I came across it again in González Faus,[103] who was inquiring what was left for liberation theology, as some people were wondering a few years ago. As far as I remember, Ellacuría did not use the formula as such. But when he proposed a *poverty-civilisation* as an expression of God's kingdom, he had the same insight; he linked the poor to the set-ting of salvation (a categorical *ubi:* outside them [apart from them]) and to the content of salvation (a substantial *quid* 'what salvation'). Moreover he recovered a central truth by earthing it in history: salvation comes from Yahweh's suffering servant. He also recovered redemption as an essential aspect of salvation: it is necessary to produce valu-able things, but it is also necessary to eradicate evils, by taking them upon our own shoulders. [104]

Let us return to our formula. As we have already said, it is counter-cultural, since the rich world thinks it already possesses 'salvation', and the means to get it, precisely because it is *not* the world of the poor. It does not occur to the rich world that salvation might come from outside, much less that it might come from the poor. Saved or damned, the rich world says, 'It's us who are real.' That is the hubris denounced by Paul.

The formula also has no defence against the objections made by history and reason. Nevertheless it is necessary, as an antidote to a society suffering from 'moral and humanitarian failure'.[105] And the fact that the *mysterium iniquitatis* is also present among the poor does not discredit the formula. The Fathers also called the Church *casta meretrix*, the 'chaste whore'. So the Church is not the setting for salvation because there is no sin in her,[106] but because of Christ's presence and the presence of his spirit in her, who will always produce life and holiness. That is a way of expressing faith. Something similar can be said about the world of the poor, even though here too faith becomes analogous. Besides their raw reality, the poor always have something of the spirit in them. And, not just as a possible but as an essential truth, the poor will always have something of Christ in them. Referring to Matthew 25, Medellín and Puebla strongly emphasised: Christ 'has wanted to identify himself very tenderly with the poorest and weakest' (n.196).[107]

5. THE MYSTERY OF THE POOR

This essay is coming to an end. But we are still left with the uneasiness we mentioned at the beginning, caused by what is novel and scandalous in our subject. We are aware of our own shortcomings. We have not offered an adequate concept of salvation.[108] We have not adequately defined the different ways in which the poor and the non-poor bring about salvation. All we have said is that the non-poor produce valuable things and knowledge for individual and communal enjoyment, on the one hand, and, on the other, the poor offer inspiration, attraction and impulse by fermentation, as they generate modest models of another kind of society. And I think we need to analyse in more depth the relationship between the needy poor and the 'poor with spirit'.

Having said this, one thing seems clear to me. There could be no salvation or humanisation if redemptive impulses did not come from the world of the poor. What the arrogant, bossy world of the non-poor produces cannot generate salvation unless, in some way or another, it passes through the world of the poor. Briefly, salvation and humanisation will come with the poor. Without the poor no human sort of salvation can come.

The uneasiness we mentioned earlier remains. We recall Ellacuría's words about the suffering servant, chosen by God to bring salvation: 'Only through a difficult act of faith can the poet of the servant discover something that looks quite the opposite in history's eyes.'[109] Likewise, only by a difficult act of faith – even when it is thoughtful faith – can we accept that there is salvation in the poor and that there is no salvation apart from them. And the reason for that is that the world of the poor confronts us with a mystery and they themselves express a mystery. There are just a few final words to say about them.

The *mysterium iniquitatis*: evil and wickedness

First and foremost – to avoid the accusation of naivety – we recognise the *mysterium iniquitatis*, that is present in the world of the poor. We see the deficiencies that bolster the selfishness of every human being, the contamination of the imagination by offerings from the North – even though the poor have every right to enjoy the benefits of civilisation that are available to them. We also see wickedness: abuse, rape, blatant machismo, deceit, mutilation, murder ... sometimes real human catastrophes.

In recent times, some of our poor people were members of the security forces and others were members of local organisations. Archbishop Romero lamented bitterly that the same thing that united them, the need to survive, was what separated them, to the point that they were killing each other. Now, to an appalling degree, the same is happening with youth gangs: people who are basically just poor people killing one another. Fourteen years after the Peace Accords in El Salvador, a country with a population of about six million, there is an average of twelve murders per day.

Mysterium iniquitatis is the tragedy of Rwanda and the Great Lakes. The North has a long-standing responsibility for this and today it is also guilty of indifference. But the African peoples are also responsible. Melquisedek Sikuli, the Congolese bishop, recognises that. He has also listed the huge problems facing his country: wretched poverty, injustice, displaced persons, raped women, sacked villages, against the background of the sin of colonialism. But he does not gloss over his compatriots' misdeeds. He gives the example of the child-soldiers, even though his compassion in the face of so much suffering moves him to seek some kind of explanation. Without defending them, he quotes some words of Kouroma from his book *Allah Is Not Pleased*: 'When you haven't got anyone in the world, no father, no mother, no sister, and you are still a child in a ruined, barbarous country, in which everyone is killing everyone else, what should you do? You become a child-soldier in order to eat and to kill: that's all you can do.'[110]

So let's have no idealisations. But don't let's have any hypocrisy either. When the rich world recalls – sometimes with a barely suppressed air of superiority – the horrors taking place in the world of the poor, aren't they avoiding taking their own atrocities seriously: Auschwitz, Hiroshima, the Gulag, Vietnam, Iraq, national security regimes? The question remains: 'Why, Lord, why?'

The *mysterium salutis*: essential holiness

However, it is also true that the poor who have suffered so much oppression and repression in our country, Central Asia, the Great Lakes; mothers grasping their children's hands and carrying all they have left on their heads, who trek hundreds of miles to seek refuge; AIDS sufferers who want to die with dignity; others struggling against various kinds of oppression: all these people are capable of resisting and celebrating.

There are stories of cruelty and misery about prisons and refugee camps. But the incredible thing is that there are also stories of love, hope, the will to live and help one another, religious and civil grassroots organisations to speak for themselves and keep their dignity. Teresa Florensa, a nun who has worked in the Great Lakes writes:

> These human beings continue to be human waste. There are millions of surplus people in our world. Nobody knows what to do with them, and they are aware that they count for nothing. They carry with them a whole history of suffering, humiliation, terror, hunger and death. Their dignity is wounded [...] But this work with the refugees in the Great Lakes is also an invitation to trust in human beings and their ability to surpass themselves under the very worst conditions.

This can shake up the non-poor of the rich world: 'What have you done to your brother?' But it should also generate respect and reverence. That will to live – live together with one another –

amidst great suffering, working to achieve this with creativity, dignity, resistance and boundless courage, defying tremendous obstacles, is what we have called essential holiness.[111] Unlike official holiness, we are not told how much freedom or necessity, virtue or obligation, grace or merit is to be found in that essential holiness. It does not have to be accompanied by heroic virtues, but it is expressed in a life that is wholly heroic. That essential holiness invites us to give to one another, receive from one another, and celebrate with one another the joy of being human.

I wonder whether the wickedness and holiness described above are like those found in the rich world. I think there are differences, at least in so far as they affect me personally. The wickedness of the world of the poor appears 'less' wicked, because they are driven to it by the need to survive and the desperation of a life of chronic poverty. There is always freedom or crumbs of freedom, one might say, but it exists amidst vulnerability, weakness, oppression by society and its institutions. The poor are those who have (nearly) all the powers of this world against them. That is why it is not easy for me to accept a *historical* symmetry between poor and non-poor, their concupiscence and the original sin they remind us of.

Moreover, holiness from below appears to be 'more' holy. To paraphrase freely some words of Kant in his *Metaphysics of Morals,* in which he distinguishes between price and worth, I think that what operates in the world of the rich, even a world that has dignity, is a culture of price, where-as what prevails in the world of poverty is worth. Jesus said the poor widow had given more than all the others, because she had given out of her poverty. She had given 'all she had'. The difference is not one of quantity but of quality. The poor have no money, so it becomes more natural for them to give themselves.

We have said that there is a disproportion between the rich man and poor Lazarus in their comparative grievance, but there is also a disproportion in their difference of dignity. Often enough the poor are the true 'shepherds of being'. Certainly they are the 'guardians of dignity', 'aristocrats of the spirit', as Jon Cortina said.

This world of the poor is what aroused Ellacuría's hopeful exultation, which was both utopian and realistic. He was well aware of the difficulties, but he also knew about 'the immense spiritual and human wealth of the poor and the Third World peoples.' Today that wealth is stifled by wretched poverty and the imposition of in some ways more developed cultural models, which are not therefore more fully human.'[112] That wealth is stifled by manifold problems but not eliminated. And sometimes it shines out radiantly.

The mystery of God in the poor

And in the poor God can be seen. In conclusion, let us express this in some of our favourite words of Gustavo Gutiérrez.

In the midst of the suffering of the innocent, he asks: 'How can we speak of God from Ayacucho?'[113] Ayacucho is a Peruvian town whose name in Quechua means 'dead man's corner'. Here those asking for God are Job, Ivan Karamazov, Jesus on the cross.

And from among the poor he answers in the well known lines of the Peruvian poet César Vallejo: 'The lottery seller who shouts "One for a thousand" contains a fathomless depth of God'.[114] Here we have the answer of the Roman centurion at the foot of the cross: 'Truly this man was Son of God' (Mk 15:39). He has found God.

The poor send us to God because God is in them, both hidden and manifest. They are 'Christ's vicars'.

On the eve of the Fifth Latin American Bishops' Conference in Aparecida, Brazil, I end this essay by offering a text of Ignacio Ellacuría, which throws light on what the Latin American churches should be and do. It is about the option for the poor. And it is also about the option of letting ourselves be saved by them:

> The great saving task is to evangelise the poor, so that in their material poverty, they may become aware and find the necessary spirit, firstly, to emerge from their poverty and oppression, secondly, to put an end to these oppressive structures, and thirdly, to create a new heaven and a new earth, where sharing outweighs accumulating, where there is time to listen and enjoy God's voice in the heart of the material world and in the heart of human history. Seeking salvation any other way is a dogmatic and historical error. If that means hoping against hope, it also means trusting firmly that all this will happen some day. The poor continue to be the world's great reservoir of human hope and spirituality.[115]

NOTES

1. In this essay we gather together ideas, sometimes whole paragraphs, that we have published over the last few years – in particular, in the following articles of the journal *Concilium*: 'Redención de la globalización. Las víctimas', 293 (2001), pp. 129–39; 'Revertir la historia', 308 (2004), pp. 811–20; 'La salvación que viene de abajo. Hacia una humanidad humanizada', 314 (2006), pp. 29–40. And also 'La opción por los pobres: dar y recibir', *Revista Latinoamericana de Teología* 69 (2006), pp. 219–61.
2. 'El desafío de las mayorías pobres', *Estudios Centroamericanos* 493–4 (1989), p.1078.
3. 'Utopía y profetismo', *Revista Latinoamericana de Teología* 17 (1989), pp. 170 ff.
4. *Ibid.*
5. *Ibid.*
6. Cf. 'El desafío' pp. 1076 ff.
7. *Ibid.*, p. 1078.
8. *Ibid.*
9. *Veo a Satán caer como el relámpago*, Barcelona, 2002, p. 209. (*I See Satan Fall Like Lightning*), Maryknoll, NY: Orbis Books, 2001).
10. *Ibid.*
11. *Ibid.* p. 210.
12. *Ibid.* p. 209.
13. 'Utopía necesaria como el pan de cada día', January, 2006.
14. 'It is threatened with death by large-scale international finance capital, that makes the market's invisible dealing the supreme and sole arbiter of history,' (J. Ziegler, UN Special Advisor on the Right to Food, in 'Entrevista', *El Pais*, 9 May 2005).
15. Current World Food Programme estimates (http://www.wfp.org/aboutwfp/facts/hunger_facts.asp). In 2002, the UN Food and Agriculture Organisation (FAO) said, 'Worldwide 840 million people are undernourished in 1998–2000.' This

figure grew to 854 million in 2001–03 (FAO, State of Food Insecurity in the World, 2006, p. 8).

16. *Ibid.* In the Old Testament *shoá* (Hebrew, Greek: *holocaustos*) is not a metaphor taken from the cultic sacrifices, in which the victim was totally destroyed. To designate these the Pentateuch uses the terms *korbán* and *'olah. Shoá* is used, after the exile, to describe the historical destruction and extermination of human beings. Luis de Sebastián has just published a book, *África, pecado de Europa* (Trotta, 2006). He uses the term 'sin', religious language, since no other civilised, democratic language appears to have the power that is needed to speak of Africa as it is.

17. *Ibid.*

18. Stockholm International Peace Research Institute (SIPRI), Yearbook 2007, Chapter 8.

19. OECD, *Agricultural Policies in OECD Countries: Monitoring and Evaluation, 2007 – Highlights* p. 38 (http://www.oecd .org/dataoecd/61/3/39524780.pdf).

20. Amnesty International Report , 2005.

21. 'To help Africa you have to understand it first. We don't want you to think for us.' From an interview in Bamako, capital of Mali, during the celebration of the World Social Forum, January 19–23, 2006. The author was born in Mali 58 years ago. She has a doctorate in social psychology and psychopathology, is a former minister of culture, consultant for the United Nations, community leader, and writer.

22. See T. Forcades i Vila, *Los crímenes de las grandes compañías farmacéuticas,* Barcelona, 2006.

23. L. de Sebastián, *Problemas de la globalización,* Barcelona, 2005, p. 4.

24. 'Today there are very few people who still say that poverty is caused by injustice' (J. Vitoria, 'Una teología de ojos abiertos. Teología y justicia. Perspectivas', *Revista Latinoamericana de Teología* 69 [2006]. And even fewer relate it to capitalism.

25. Yves Calvez spoke recently about 'the silences of the Church's social doctrine.' Referring to these, José Comblin states that this doctrine 'does not question the system'. It criticises what is referred to in the adjectives, such as savage capitalism, but not capitalism itself. John Paul II's encyclical *Laborem Exercens* did deal with the question; he stated that labour was the fundamental principle of economics and anthropology (see the commentary of I. Ellacuría, 'Conflicto entre trabajo y capital en la presente fase histórica. Un análisis de la Encíclica de Juan Pablo II sobre el trabajo humano', *Estudios Centroamericanos* 409 [1982], pp. 1008–24). This papal

insight did not make it into the Church's public discourse, probably because of its resemblance to the thought of Marx, especially during the 1980s, when Reagan was determined to crush the revolutionary movements in Nicaragua, El Salvador and Guatemala. Politically, any outright questioning of capitalism was considered to be going too far. Thus the Church's social doctrine was co-opted. Ellacuría had already said that, whereas the Church's social doctrine aimed more at (merely) moderating capitalism, liberation theology aimed more at humanising socialism.

26. *La oración de San Francisco*, Santander, 1999, p. 98.
27. '¿Quién manda en el mundo?', in *Servicios Koinonía*, 20 January 2006. UNDP Human Development Report, 1997, p. 30: 'It is estimated that the additional cost of achieving and maintaining universal access to basic education for all, basic health care of all, reproductive health care for all women, adequate food for all, and safe water and sanitation for all is roughly $40 billion a year. That is less than 4% of the combined wealth of the 225 richest people in the world.'
28. We have piled up enough quotes to make our case. Please forgive the author for not always being able to give the precise sources from which they are taken.
29. 'Today an estimated 30% of humanity live in dire poverty, which is much less than in earlier times, when it might have been 80 or 90% of the total. But it is also true that the kings, nobles, bankers, and landlords of the past were economic pygmies compared to the rich people of today. Modern societies are becoming ever more divided societies (two societies in one). They are made up of two separate groups whose lives are far apart, with very different standards of living and very different ways of using those societies' material goods and culture. [...] The current difference between wealth and poverty is more extreme than it has ever been before in history. [...] The inequality would not be so terrible if the worse off were living decently . The disgusting thing is they are not even doing that.' L. de Sebastián, *Problemas de la globalización*, cit., pp. 2–4.
30. Leonardo Boff comments: 'I am frankly alarmed at the catastrophe that will result from the entrance of this giant into the capitalist circuit, which is characterised not only by exploitation of people, but also by destruction of the environment.'
31. According to deputies of the Chinese Communist Party, 80 per cent of Chinese businesses do not offer their workers contracts. And with the 20 per cent that do, the contract is for less than one year. The 'Chinese economic miracle' is doing

serious harm: corruption and a massively widening income gap. In fact, Chinese development has often eroded labour standards and destroyed jobs in other countries, especially in the Third World. Something similar could occur with India. 'If we were ever found talking in a group the supervisors would threaten us with the idea of the plant being closed, "If you don't reach the production targets then all this work will go to China," they said.' Lupe, electronics worker, Mexico in *Clean up your computer: working conditions in the electronics sector,* CAFOD, London, 2004. p. 2. http://www.cafod.org.uk/var/storage/original/application/phpYyhizc.pdf

32. Allow me to use words written by K. Rahner in a completely different context. In the 1960s, given the deplorable situation of the dogmatic theology then in use, in his first great article on the Trinity, he attacked the way the doctrine was then approached: 'It can be seen to be wrong simply by observing its effective reality: *it can't be like this.*' ('Advertencias sobre el tratado dogmático *De Trinitate*' in *Escritos de Teología* IV, Madrid, 1962, p.117). John XXIII wanted to say something similar before the Council when he asked for 'the church's windows to be thrown open'. Inside the Church you couldn't breathe any fresh air.

33. See A. Nolan's magnificent book *God in South Africa* (Grand Rapids, MI: William B,. Eermans, 1988).

34. H. Marcuse said this many years ago in *One-Dimensional Man.*

35. I. Ellacuría, 'Discernir "el signo" de los tiempos', *Diakonía* 17 (1981), p. 58.

36. The critique of democracy is an important long-term task. Here we point out that Ellacuría regarded the mere assessment of its procedures as inadequate. Democracy has to be understood as a form of government that seeks the common good, the necessary basis for establishing a society that is inclusive, just and in solidarity with the least well off. This means that democracy raises not only political but also social and economic issues that are equally important. Briefly, a social democracy is one that makes it possible to change the unjust conditions in which the majority of people live. Accordingly, Ellacuría thought that democracy has meaning only in so far as it is based on the reality of the poor majorities, those large impoverished sectors that are excluded by the dominant groups. That is what must be checked. If the assessment is not positive, there is not much sense in talking about democracy.

37. Here are some examples: According to Kofi Annan (1999):

'Official development aid is at its lowest level for the last fifty years.' 'Western aid to the Third World has simply decreased, and I regard that as a crime,' said James Wolfenson, former president of the World Bank (2000). Flavio Miragaya Perri, Brazil's ambassador to the FAO, speaks of an original sin, committed by the colonial powers from time immemorial. And he adds: 'First World aid to combat hunger and poverty (around 50 billion dollars annually) is equal to one-seventh of the subsidies that are given to their farmers (350 billion dollars) to grow cheaper products that have a competitive advantage in the market', (taken from *Co-Latino*, San Salvador, 1 June 2004). Since 2005, however, aid has increased but the world's richest countries are still failing to fulfil the pledges they made at the G8 meeting in 2005.

38. 'Many poor countries, especially those in Africa, will miss the Millennium Development Goals by a large margin. But neither African inaction nor a lack of aid will necessarily be the reason. Instead, responsibility for near-certain "failure" lies with the overly-ambitious goals themselves and unrealistic expectations placed on aid.' *What's Wrong with the Millennium Development Goals?* Michael Clemens and Todd Moss; Center for Global Development, Washington D.C.; September 2005. (www.cgdev.org/files/3940_file_WWMGD .pdf)

39. Figure given in the demonstration against poverty in Madrid on 21 October 2006.

40. *Op. cit.* And Irene Khan, director of Amnesty International, says that 'governments are losing their moral compass' (11 September 2001).

41. Likewise, we should not trivialise the feast of the 'Holy Innocents' or just treat it as a decorative detail of our Christmas liturgy. Whether the story is historical or not, it is about innocent babies cruelly murdered.

42. This refers to an incident in which a general and landlord ordered his dogs to be set upon an eight-year-old child (one child) who had flung a stone and injured the paw of his favourite dog: 'I would rather remain with my unavenged suffering and unsatisfied indignation, even if I were wrong. Besides, too high a price is asked for harmony; it's beyond our means to pay so much to enter on it. And so I hasten to give back my entrance ticket, and if I am an honest man I am bound to give it back as soon as possible. And that I am doing. It's not God that I don't accept, Alyosha, only I most respectfully return him the ticket.'

43. Remember that for Plato the sphere is the symbol of perfection (*Symposium* XIV–XV, 189c–192d).

44. The Cristianisme i Justicia Foundation published a pamphlet with the title, *¿Mundialización o conquista?*, Barcelona, 1999.
45. 'Progreso y precipicio. Recuerdos del futuro del mundo moderno', *Revista Latinoamericana de Teología* 54 (2001), p. 302. My italics.
46. L. de Sebastián, 'Europa: globalización y pobreza', *Concilium* 293 (2001), p. 743. More recently he wrote: 'I understand globalisation to be the result – albeit still partial and not unstoppable – of a process that tends to consolidate national markets for goods and services [...] within great world markets. Meanwhile market logic (privatisation) increasingly takes over spheres and activities of humanity's social life.' (*Problemas de la globalización*, p. 28).
47. *Ibid.* p. 4.
48. 'Europa', p. 743.
49. In *Carta a las Iglesias* 544 (2005), p. 11.
50. Taken from *Zenit*, 23 January 2006.
51. Words of González Calvo, director of the magazine *Mundo Negro*.
52. '... there has been a clear trend over the past two decades towards rising inequality within countries. Of the 73 countries for which data is available, 53, with more than 80 per cent of the world's population, have seen inequality rise, while only 9 (with 4 per cent of the population) have seen it narrow.' – *UNDP Human Development Report*, 2005. p. 55.
53. www.marca.es/futbol/champions 12 February 2001.
54. John Paul II, *Pastores Gregis*, 16 October 2003, no. 67. My italics.
55. F. Mayor Zaragoza, 'Tener presente el futuro', *El País*, 6 June 2006.
56. H. Pinter, Acceptance speech for the Nobel Prize for Literature, 7 December 2005.
57. J. Taubes, interview published in *Messianesimo e cultura. Saggi di politica, teologia e storia*, Milan, 2001, pp. 399–400.
58. 'El desafío', p. 1080.
59. The formula is present, in a way, in Marx: salvation comes from a social class at the bottom of history. I. Ellacuría agrees ('El pueblo crucificado', in *Conversión de la Iglesia al reino de Dios*, San Salvador, 1986, pp. 29-31), although we should recall that Marxism does not see saving potential in the *lumpenproletariat*. I do not think the social philosophy that is the basis of democracy addresses the issue either. At most, it offers the poor citizenship with the same rights as others, but it does not place them, either in theory or in practice, at the centre of society. It does not make the poor *as such* the specific bringers of salvation. Neither does the Church do so, either in theory or in practice.

60. Przywara stresses this. Reality is always greater than our ideas. The greater the reality, the more respectful of it our ideas should be. So the *via negativa* need not be an expression of lack of knowledge about reality, but may well express respect and humility – and a more profound knowledge of it.

61. Interview in *Éxodo* 78–79 (2005), p. 66.

62. 'El poder, ¿para qué?, ¿para quiénes?' *Páginas* 194 (2005), pp. 50–61.

63. 'Golpeando suavemente los recursos locales de la esperanza', *Concilium* 308 (2004), p. 104.

64. 'Las bienaventuranzas, carta fundacional de la Iglesia de los pobres', in *Conversión de la Iglesia al Reino de Dios*, San Salvador, 1985, pp. 129–51.

65. 'Misión actual de la Compañía de Jesús', *Revista Latinoamericana de Teología* 29 (1993), pp. 119 ff.

66. A. Pieris, 'Cristo más allá del dogma. Hacer cristología en el contexto de las religiones de los pobres' (I), *Revista Latinoamericana de Teología* 52 (2001), p. 16.

67. 'Iglesia y solidaridad con los pobres de África', in *Identidad africana y cristiana*, Estella, 1999, pp. 273ff.

68. He gave a lot of thought to this in his final years. See 'Misión actual de la Compañía de Jesús', *Revista Latinoamericana de Teología* 29 (1993), pp. 115–26 [the text was written in 1981]; 'El reino de Dios y el paro en el Tercer Mundo', *Concilium* 180 (1982), pp. 588–96; 'Utopía y profetismo desde América Latina. Un ensayo concreto de soteriología histórica', *Revista Latinoamericana de Teología* 17 (1989), pp. 141–84.

69. 'La misión en la Iglesia latinoamericana actual', *Revista Latinoamericana de Teología* 68 (2006), p. 191. As well as this, the author stresses that the poor come first for the mission.

70. I. Ellacuría, 'Lectura latinoamericana de los *ejercicios espirituales* de San Ignacio', *Revista Latinoamericana de Teología* 23 (1991), p. 132.

71. See what I wrote in *Jesucristo liberador. Lectura histórico-teológica de Jesús de Nazaret*, San Salvador, 1991, pp. 220–3, y Madrid, 2001; ET, *Jesus the Liberator: A HistoricalTheological View* (Maryknoll, NY: Orbis Books, 1992). What I wrote was also inspired by I. Ellacuría, 'Pobres', in *Conceptos fundamentales de pastoral*, Madrid, 1983, pp. 786–802.

72. Puebla mentions this in no. 1142, in speaking of God's option for the poor and the reasons for it, but we believe it is equally valid for describing the potential of the poor to motivate conversion.

73. Adorno says, 'It is necessary to set up perspectives in which the world appears disrupted, alienated, showing its cracks

and tears, beggarly and deformed,' *Minima Moralia*, Madrid, 1987, p. 250.

74. Bonhoeffer says that in the presence of Lazarus a miracle can occur: 'What the rich man has not seen, that his world is a world of death', quoted in M. Zechmeister, 'Grito y canto', *Revista Latinoamericana de Teología* 69 (2006).

75. 'Desafío' p. 1076.

76. P. Casaldáliga, 'Del desencanto inmediatista a la utopía esperanzada', *Concilium* 311 (2005), p. 156.

77. 'Quinto centenario de América Latina. ¿Descubrimiento o encubrimiento?', *Revista Latinoamericana de Teología* 21 (1990), p. 282.

78. To these three points made by Ellacuría, we usually add a fourth: 'letting reality bear us'. And that happens in the world of the poor.

79. 'Pobres', p. 796. Puebla also speaks of the effective political value of the poor: 'They have begun to organise in order to live their whole faith, and therefore also to claim their rights' (Puebla, no. 1137). And it comments: 'Thus faith makes them a political liberating force.'

80. I have analysed this in greater detail in 'Bearing with One Another in Faith: A Theological Analysis of Christian Solidarity,' in *The Principle of Mercy* (Maryknoll, NY: Orbis Books, 1994), pp. 144–72.

81. 'Palabras en el doctorado *Honoris Causa* en Ciencias políticas al Presidente de Costa Rica Dr. Óscar Arias', mimeographed text. [Speech given at the conferral of the doctorate *honoris causa* in Political Sciences upon the President of Costa Rica, Dr Oscar Arias.]

82. See what I wrote in *Jesus the Liberator*, pp. 219–32.

83. C. Díaz, *Monseñor Óscar Romero*, Madrid, 1999, pp. 95–6.

84. In 'Teología cristiana después de Auschwitz', *Concilium* 195 (1984), pp. 214 ff. It is important to note that today the victims of Auschwitz are still remembered, and they are remembered so that we may find salvation in them. We also remember D. Bonhoeffer, E. Stein and E. Hillesum.

85. Taken from J. Vitoria, 'Una teología de ojos abiertos'.

86. Quote from a nun who has spent many years in the Great Lakes region.

87. The most detailed account can be found in 'América Latina: lugar de pecado, lugar de perdón', *Concilium* 204 (1986), p. 226.

88. See what I wrote in 'Jesuanic Martyrs in the Third World,' in *Witnesses to the Kingdom: The Martyrs of El Salvador and the Crucified Peoples* (Maryknoll, NY: Orbis Books, 2003), pp. 119–32.

89. Regarding the salvation the martyrs offer the Church, see my essay, 'The Latin American Martyrs: Challenge and Grace for the Church,' in *Witnesses*, pp. 134–54.

90. Listen to Moltmann's criticism: 'It seems to me that it is not correct to speak of the "crucified people" who "take away the sin of the world" and thus "redeem" the world. All that does is use religion to glorify and perpetuate the people's suffering. The people do not want to save the world by their suffering, but to be redeemed from their suffering and have a humanly dignified life', 'Teología Latinoamericana', in L. C. Susin, ed., *El mar se abrió*, Santander, 2001, p. 209. His last sentence seems right to me, but that does not necessarily make it untrue that the poor, just by being poor, bring salvation into history. Where I would be in agreement with Moltmann is in rejecting any mechanical relation between suffering and salvation.

91. J. Vitoria, *op. cit.*

92. Taken from M. Zechmeister, *op. cit.*

93. This has been said by Boff and Casaldáliga. Even with all the evils it produces, present-day globalisation is in fact laying the foundations for a future globalisation with great human potential.

94. Enrique Álvarez Córdova, a Salvadoran oligarch and landlord, distributed his lands to peasants on the condition that the land was owned and worked cooperatively. He struggled for agrarian reform in his country and entered the ranks of the Democratic Revolutionary Front as a political member, not as a combatant. He was killed in 1979. A brilliant example of analogy.

95. *Church: The Human Story of God*, New York, 1990, p. 12.

96. This does not mean that the understanding of the traditional formula had not been evolving right from the start. The formula could – and did – lead to rigorism, although in the beginning, and beyond the Councils which did not fall into rigorism (Fourth Lateran and Florence, 1442), there appeared the common Christian understanding that God willed all to be saved. One theological solution was to postulate the existence of the Church even before Christ, and thus was forged the theological maxim: *Ecclesia ab Abel*. Church? Yes, from Abel on, that is, from an innocent victim, the just one, the believer (Matt 23:25; Heb 11:4). Cf. C. Susin, '*Ecclesia ab Abel*. Los "pobres" y la Iglesia al inicio del siglo XXI', *Concilium* 314 (2006), pp. 59–69. Thus membership of the Church may be understood by *analogy*, but on a basic criterion: wherever there are just people, innocent victims, believers, like Abel –

there, *in some way*, there is Church, and there is salvation.

97. According to *Dignitatis Humanae*, any human reality can be a setting for salvation.

98. According to *Gaudium et Spes* 3, salvation is all-pervasive: 'It is human persons [body and soul, heart and conscience, intellect and will] that must be saved. [...] It is human society that must be renewed.'

99. A. Pieris, 'El Vaticano II: un concilio "generador de crisis" con una agenda no escrita', *Revista Latinoamericana de Teología* 67 (2006), p. 43: 'The best fruit of this crisis-generating decision [the biblical soteriology rediscovered in the Council] was liberation theology, which was created by the poor of Latin America in the process of hearing and responding to the Word, as they heard it in the scriptures and in the history of their time. That was a long-overdue discovery – of an alternative to the domination theology that a non-biblical scholastic theology had produced.'

100. *Discourse in Louvain*, 2 February 1980. Though not literally, Romero also stressed the second part of Irenaeus's saying: *Gloria autem hominis visio Dei*. He said: 'No one knows himself who has not found God. [...] How I wish, beloved brothers and sisters, that as a result of my preaching today, each one of us may find God!" (Homily of 10 February 1980, delivered two weeks before his assassination).

101. *Marx y la Biblia*, Salamanca, 1972, p. 82.

102. *¿Todavía la salvación cristiana?* II, pp. 662, 702–03, 731–2. See also 'La soteriología histórica: un modelo a partir de la teología salvadoreña (I)', *Revista Latinoamericana de Teología* 33 (1994), p. 292: 'The poor become the ideal setting for liberating saving action to bring about God's kingdom.' He mentions it again in the article quoted from this same issue.

103. Because liberation theology thinks in terms of the poor, it can 'paraphrase a well-known ancient saying: *extra pauperes nulla salus*' ('Una tarea histórica: de la liberación a la apocalíptica', *Sal Terrae* [October 1995], p. 718).

104. Thinking specifically of the university, he said: 'In one way or another, Christianity sees the most needy as the redeemers of history.' ('Diez años después, ¿es posible una universidad distinta?', *Estudios Centroamericanos* 324–5 [1975], p. 627). And in 1979 he stated it explicitly: 'The most explicit witness to the Christian inspiration of the UCA is whether it is serving the people and whether in that service it lets itself be guided by the oppressed people themselves', ('Las funciones fundamentales de la Universidad y su

operativización', in *Planteamiento universitario*, 1989, p. 120). His first point is accepted, at least theoretically: a university's option for the poor. The second is bolder: a university should allow itself to be guided by the poor.

105. I. Ellacuría, 'Utopía', p. 173.

106. According to *Gaudium et Spes* 19, even believers, 'through the deficiencies of their religious, moral and social life, have concealed more than revealed the true face of God and of religion' and are one of the causes of atheism.

107. The language used here by Puebla is stronger than: 'he has not left us, but lives among us', which it also uses to mention the presence of Christ 'in the midst of his Church, principally in the Holy Eucharist and in the proclamation of his word; he is present among those who come together in his name and also in the person of the pastors he has sent' (*ibid.*).

108. That is the criticism made by J.Costadoat in his article 'La liberación en la cristología de Jon Sobrino', *Teología y Vida* XLV (2004), pp. 62–84. ET. 'Central Ideas in Jon Sobrino's Christology' in *Hope and Solidarity: Jon Sobrino's Challenge to Christian Theology, ed.* Stephen J. Pope, Orbis Books, New York 2008.

109. 'El pueblo crucificado. Ensayo de soteriología histórica', *Revista Latinoamericana de Teología* 18 (1989), p. 326.

110. See the complete text in *Concilium* 293 (2001), pp. 145–6.

111. Cf. *Where is God? Earthquake, Terrorism, Barbarity, and Hope* (Maryknoll, NY: Orbis Books, 2004), pp. 71–105.

112. 'Misión actual', pp. 119 ff.

113. 'Cómo hablar de Dios desde Ayacucho', *Revista latinoamericana de Teologia* 15 (1988), pp. 233–41.

114. Cited in G. Gutiérrez, *El Dios de la vida*, Salamanca, 1994, p. 174. ET: *The God of Life* (Maryknoll, NY: Orbis Books, 1991).

115. 'Pobres', p. 797.